Meena Pathak's **Flavors of India**

Meena Pathak's
Flavors

# of India

NEW HOLLAND

Contents

The recipes

Introduction

Food has always been a great passion of mine. Some of my earliest memories are of going to the market with my grandmother in Bombay (now called Mumbai) and watching her haggle with the vegetable sellers to get the best produce—how impressed I was! In her house, food was always something that was eaten for taste and enjoyment, not just for nourishment. I can't remember when I first became interested in cooking... it now seems like second nature. As a child I would beg my grandmother's cook to let me help out in the kitchen. Often, I would just sit and watch, but gradually I was allowed to help with chopping and preparing and, by the age of ten, I was happily going to the market and helping to cook meals for the family. I grew up in Bombay but, because my father was in the Indian army, I was able to spend holidays with my parents wherever he happened to be posted. In time, I learned about the regional differences of India and I soon discovered a whole new world of ingredients, flavors, and recipes.

When I finished school I decided to study food technology and hotel management, and was determined to have a career in the food industry. However, things don't always work out the way you plan them and out of the blue I had a marriage proposal, via my aunt. I was fiercely opposed to the idea, but agreed to consider it and, before I knew it,

I was engaged to a young man named Kirit Pathak, who was visiting India with his father. I didn't know much about what his family did—I thought they owned some shops in England, but I knew that I would shortly be going there.

At the age of twenty, I left for England, quite unaware of what was ahead of me. I was more than surprised when I discovered that the family business was Patak's (they dropped the "h"). They made authentic Indian snacks and pickles and sold them throughout the UK. I remember the first time I visited the Patak's factory with my husband... my inquisitive mind was asking hundreds of questions about where the fresh produce came from, what spice blends they used, and so on. I launched myself into the business with enthusiasm, determined to use my experience and knowledge and love of food. I talked to people and visited Indian restaurants and was amazed by what people in England viewed as Indian food. It became my mission to share the real flavors of India, and now, twenty-five years on, I am delighted to have written my first book. These are some of my favorite recipes and I hope that, like me, you will be inspired to create your own flavors.

Meera Pathak

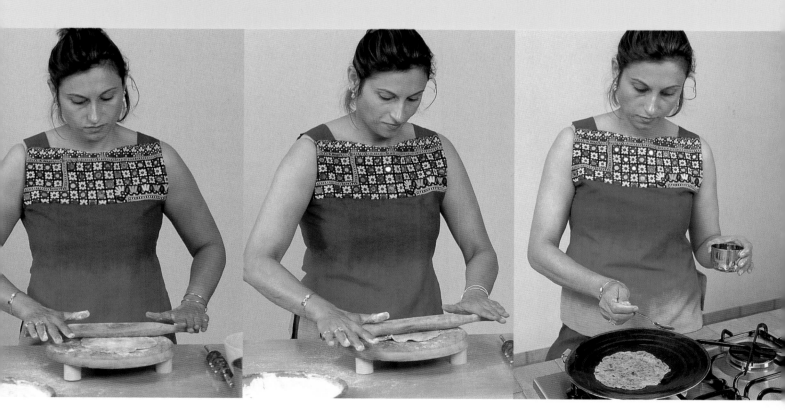

India's culinary traditions

INDIA, my homeland, is a vast subcontinent that is made up of several states, all with their own unique cooking traditions and tastes. India has a multilayered culture, with a population of one billion, five major faiths, numerous languages and dialects, and a rich heritage. Indian food is a reflection of this heritage and is shaped by the culture and religious beliefs of the people. The regionality of the cuisine is also affected by the vastly differing landscapes that influence what can be grown. The climate is also a factor—in the colder northern states, warming, aromatically spiced dishes are eaten, whereas in the intense heat of southern India, the food is lighter and uses more coconut and black pepper.

The regions of India

I only began to appreciate the diversity of the regions of India when I started traveling in my summer holidays, visiting the places where my father, who was in the army, was posted. I remember visiting an army camp in the far north of India and catching my first glimpse of the snow-capped peaks of the Himalayan mountain range. The breathtaking valley of Kashmir has lush meadows and is where India's saffron is grown. Its lakes are beautiful and sailing on the famous Dal lake is a truly romantic experience. It is cool enough to rear sheep, which is why lamb or mutton is used extensively in Kashmiri dishes, and this is where I had my first taste of meat. Apple and apricot orchards dot the countryside and black cumin seeds grow wild. The world-famous basmati rice grows in the foothills of the Himalayas. The soil here is fertile and irrigated by the phosphorous-rich waters of the Ganges—the river is icy cold, but if you're brave enough for a quick dip it is wonderfully refreshing.

The state of Punjab in the northwest is one of the most fertile, due to the fact that it is irrigated by five major rivers. Although rice does grow here, the staple diet is wheat. Traveling through Punjab you come across tiny villages where the food is still cooked in earthenware pots over open fires. The food from Punjab has become very popular in restaurants abroad—the classic dishes such as tandooris, tikkas, naan, and lassi all come from Punjab. The best food can be found in small roadside restaurants where the menus are basic, but the food is delicious and fresh. A regional specialty is Kaali dal, made from black urad dal and kidney beans slowly simmered with cinnamon, garlic, and cloves. The only accompaniment you need is some bread and a large glass of freshly churned lassi.

To the east, lie the fertile plains of Bengal. The coastal area is lined with coconut palms and the fields covered with mustard plantations. An abundance of fish is eaten in this region. My travels also took me north of Bengal to the sloping tea plantations in the Assam hills, where the cool air and seasonal rains make the climate ideal for growing the famous Darjeeling tea.

This page and opposite: **The sights of India are often breathtaking and this vibrancy is reflected in Indian cooking. Colors are everywhere, from traditionally decorated trucks to the day's catch in Cochin to lush tea plantations in Kerala.**

To the west lies the Malabar coast and this is the area that I associate with home. My family originally came from Gujarat, but I grew up in my grandmother's house in Bombay (now called Mumbai), the cosmopolitan capital of Maharashtra. Goa, to the south, is where I spent many holidays as a teenager, eating my entire quota of fish cooked with spices and coconut, and drinking feni, a drink made from cashew nuts. Gujarat, Maharashtra, and Goa are all strikingly different, but I was lucky living in Bombay where I could experience the contrasts. The Deccan plateau is in the heart of Maharashtra and the cotton for our clothes was grown in the cotton fields here. On visits to my aunt's sugarcane plantation we used to stop and pick peanuts off the trees and see the millet and barley being harvested—if we were lucky we would catch the sounds of local workers singing folk songs as they worked.

South India is lush and green with a maze of small rivers. Food here is very different to that cooked in the rest of India. Rice and fish are the staples, while flavors such as curry leaves, black pepper, asafoetida, and coconut are fundamental to most south Indian dishes.

Influences from abroad

Though India is one of the oldest civilizations it has been enriched over the centuries by other invading cultures. The most important is probably the Mughal invasion in the sixteenth century. This had a profound effect on the country and its cuisine. The Muslim conquerors brought their favorite dishes and cooking methods to the north Indian states and the fusion of these with Indian staples and local foods led to the evolution of Mughlai cuisine. Meat was introduced and transformed into delicate kormas, spicy kabobs, and fragrant biryanis. However, the influence was concentrated mainly in the north. This is because it was relatively easy to invade the north via the Khyber Pass, and also because the northern states enjoyed a similar climate to the invaders' home countries. South India was seen as relatively isolated and because of this, it has remained predominantly vegetarian.

The Parsis arrived in India in the seventh century after fleeing religious persecution in Iran, and settled on the coast of Gujarat. The Parsi community remains a small one, for they pledged not to spread their religion or to intermarry. They have nonetheless contributed significantly to Indian culture, and I have included some of my favorite Parsi dishes in this book.

The Portuguese were the first colonizers of India in 1498 and the last to leave in 1961, and their mark has most certainly been left on the cuisine of Goa, where they arrived. Fish is a favorite, as well as pork vindaloo, a Goan signature dish famous for its searing heat.

The influence of religion on food

Although more than 80 percent of Indians are Hindu, there are several other important religions. Muslims account for about 12 percent of the population, the remainder being Christians, Buddhists, and Parsis. In Hinduism there are five main castes. Each has different food taboos and customs, but in the broadest sense, all Hindus avoid eating beef, because the cow is considered sacred in Indian mythology. Certain Hindus are strict vegetarians, which means they avoid fish, shellfish, and eggs, as well as meat and poultry. Some very strict vegetarians won't even eat tomatoes or watermelons because their colors resemble that of meat. However, many middle-class Hindus eat meat in restaurants and non-Hindu homes. The Bengali Hindus will eat sacrificial meat and fish.

Muslims make up a sizeable part of the population, and from this community come most Indian meat dishes. Muslims have some forbidden foods, notably pork. Alcohol is also forbidden, although some Muslims bend the rules.

Indian Christians have virtually no food taboos, but some avoid meat on Fridays and cut back on certain foods during Lent. Perhaps the most restrictive diet belongs to the Jains, who practice ultravegetarianism. That can make life very difficult for the cook!

Fasting and feasting

There are over 20 major feast days in the Hindu calendar and probably as many fast days. People fast on special days for different gods. Rather than avoiding all food, fasting involves taking a vow of self-denial. However, there are certain foods that are very definitely forbidden on these days, such as meat, alcohol and, in certain regions, rice. The whole process is quite complicated because of the regional differences. As a child I used to think of the food cooked on those fasting days as celebration food. Although

Above, left to right: **Garlands made of flowers are often part of the prayer ritual; traditional Kathakali dancers in Cochin; women collecting water from a standpipe in Chennai.**

we did not "fast" we wanted to eat the food cooked for those who were fasting. The food for fasting days includes nuts, potatoes, fruits, certain vegetables, sago, milk, yogurt, paneer, coconut, and root vegetables. Food would always be cooked in ghee during fasting. In very strict families the kitchen is washed clean before the food is cooked, and a small prayer ceremony is conducted before the meal is eaten.

There are hundreds of reasons to celebrate in India, whether it is a harvest celebration, a god's day, or a special date in the Hindu calendar. Food plays an important part in these celebrations, along with gifts and prayers. The most widely celebrated festival is Diwali, the Festival of Lights, which takes place every year in October or November. It is the beginning of the Hindu New Year and is a time when a lot of festive food is prepared, particularly desserts. The preparations start a month in advance and many Indians spring-clean their houses to symbolize a new beginning. It's a time for reflection and charity. It is also the beginning of the financial year, so you might pray to the goddess of wealth or make offerings of silver and gold.

Foods for healing

For centuries Indians have believed that food should be eaten not only for taste, but also to help cure physical and mental ailments. Ayurveda is the science of diet, healing, and health. It is the most widely practiced form of medicine in India and many Indian cooks have an instinct for what ingredients to add to a dish to help alleviate certain problems. Increasingly, this way of eating is being explored in other parts of the world. Food plays an important part in our lives and therefore the chemical balance provided by what we eat aids healing and promotes good health and well-being.

Ayurvedic healers believe there are six basic tastes—sweet, sour, salty, pungent, bitter, and astringent—and each of these tastes helps in healing specific problems.

Sweet	soothing, nourishing, energizing, and satisfying
Sour	increases appetite, helps digestion, produces saliva
Salty	increases water intake, gives the skin a glow, cures stiffness
Pungent	increases blood circulation, kills worms in the upper and lower digestive tracts, purifies the mouth
Bitter	blood purifier, firms the skin, and is an antidote to poison
Astringent	aids digestion, blood purifier.

The following foods and spices are believed to help alleviate certain conditions:

■ **Black cumin, fish, eggs, figs, sesame seeds, sweet potatoes, mangoes, ghee, sago**
Help subdue wind in the body
■ **Buttermilk, cucumber, zucchini, lemons, oranges, radish, spinach, water, sunflower seeds,**
Help subdue bile in the body
■ **Dates, alcohol, eggplants, fenugreek, ginger, honey, onions, tea, salt, pickles, lentils**
Help subdue the production of mucus

My favorite ingredients

Ajowan (ajwain)

Ajowan seeds are very similar in appearance to cumin seeds and have a strong, distinctive flavor that resembles aniseed. The spice is used to add a zing to many fish and vegetable dishes, as well as some flour-based snacks. Chewed on their own, ajowan seeds might help alleviate a stomachache as well as diarrhea and colic. The spice comes from a herbaceous plant closely related to caraway, which has feathery leaves, flowers and tiny seeds. These seeds, when dried, are the spice.

Asafoetida (hing)

Asafoetida has a very overpowering, almost unpleasant smell, which is calmed when it is fried in oil. It is often added to dals to alleviate wind. Asafoetida is made from a dried gum resin that is taken from the roots of a perennial plant native to Kashmir. The dried resin is ground to a yellowish powder that is used in small quantities in cooking in a variety of lentil and vegetable dishes.

Eggplant (baingan or brinjal)

Eggplants are the fruits of a plant originally cultivated in India, but now grown in warm climates throughout the world. They come in all different shapes, sizes, and colors, from deep purple, green, or even white-skinned ones. They are always eaten cooked and can be made into a hot pickle, sliced and deep-fried for a tasty snack, or made into a spicy curry.

Bay leaf (tej patta)

These are the leaves of the evergreen bay tree, used in Indian cooking in their dried form. The leaves are generally added to hot oil at the beginning of a dish to release their sweet, delicate aroma.

Cardamom (elaichi)

Cardamom has a delicate, aromatic fragrance, which is used to flavor meat and vegetable dishes, as well as desserts and drinks. It is an essential ingredient in garam masala (see page 22). Cardamom is the dried fruit of a plant native to India. It takes the form of a pod containing brown seeds, which can be ground to a fine powder or used whole. You can also use cracked whole pods in cooking. There are several varieties and you will see brown cardamom pods as well as the pale green ones, but the green ones have a much finer flavor.

Cassia (jungli dalchini)

Often confused with cinnamon, cassia bark is harder and coarser and with an inferior flavor. It is used in much the same way as cinnamon.

Chat masala

Chat masala is a spice mix, usually made with salt and pepper, cumin seeds, ground ginger, and dried mango. Look for it in Asian grocers.

Chilies, dried (lal mirch)

There are a confusing number of chili varieties, but the most commonly used dried chilies in Indian cooking are the small, red ones—they will add a fiery heat to any dish. They can be used whole, crushed, flaked, or ground. Remove the seeds before using to lessen the heat.

Chilies, fresh (hari mirch)

I generally use the long, thin green chilies when fresh ones are called for, although they can vary in heat so use with caution. The seeds can be removed to make them less fiery. They form an essential part of many pastes, including the one given on page 20. Always wash your hands after handling chilies.

Cinnamon (dalchini)

The spice used in cooking is the dried inner bark of the cinnamon tree, an evergreen native to Sri Lanka. It is one of the most important and earliest known spices, and is an essential ingredient of garam masala. It is used in its "stick" form, as well as a ground spice. Its warm, sweet aroma enhances rice dishes, as well as meat dishes and desserts. In Ayurvedic medicine, it is used to alleviate headaches, colds, and rheumatic pains. Cinnamon bark infused in hot water is a soothing drink for a sore throat.

Cloves (long)

Cloves are the small, dried buds of the clove tree that have a sweet aroma, but a bitter taste. They are used to flavor rice and savory dishes, and are also used in spice mixtures, including garam masala.

Above: **A vegetable seller displays an array of produce, including tomatoes, okra, eggplants, tapioca, and beans.**

Coconut (narial)

Coconut palms grow in abundance all over southern India. The white flesh is used fresh or dried and shredded, either as a garnish or in chutneys and pastes. Creamed coconut is used as a base for curries, and coconut milk is used in both sweet and savory dishes. Its delicate flavor enhances fish and chicken curries, as well as vegetable dishes. Coconut milk can be bought in cans, as powder, or in block form (reconsitute with water). Coconut water, the liquid inside coconuts, is used mainly for drinks.

Cilantro
(hara dhaniya)
Fresh green cilantro is used as a herb and has quite a different aroma to the dried coriander seeds from the same plant. It makes a wonderful garnish . Generally, recipes usually call for only the leaves to be used but I use the stems wherever I can—they are great thrown into soups and sauces.

Coriander seeds (dhaniya)
The pungent, slightly sweet, citrus flavor of coriander seeds is used in vegetable, meat, fish, and poultry dishes. The seeds come from a leafy herb bearing lacy flowers—these seeds are dried and used extensively, whole or ground, as an aromatic spice in Indian cooking. The whole seeds are often dry-roasted and then coarsely crushed with other spices to make a spice mixture. The flavor of the ground spice is not as intense as that of whole seeds.

Cumin (jeera)
The distinctive aroma of cumin seeds is used to flavor rice and curries. Cumin seeds are the fruits of a small annual herb, which grows throughout India. They are used dried, and range in color from light, greenish brown to dark brown. They can be fried in hot oil to intensify their flavor or dry-roasted and then ground with other spices. Ground cumin is available from supermarkets, but it quickly loses its flavor. Another variety of cumin is black cumin (kala jeera), although black cumin is less aromatic and not as bitter in flavor.

Curry leaves (kari patta)
This aromatic herb is used to add flavor to many dishes, particularly in southern India, but it also has medicinal properties and can ease stomach pains. Despite its name, it does not have the flavor of curry and is actually related to the lemon family. Curry leaves are fried in hot oil to bring out their nutty flavor. They are readily available in Asian grocers and are best used fresh, because dried curry leaves have only a fraction of the flavor. I often freeze curry leaves—first wash them and then dry them on dish towels. Then simply put them into a bag and place in the freezer. They will lose some of their colour, but none of the flavor.

Fennel seeds (saunf)
Dried fennel seeds are used throughout India, not only to add a sweet, aniseed flavor to a variety of dishes, but also as a mouth freshener. They are similar in appearance to cumin seeds, although greener in color. Fennel is used as a digestive aid, and is also thought to relieve wheezing, catarrh, and asthma.

Fenugreek (methi)
Fenugreek is used to flavor a variety of dishes and is also used in bread making. It is one of the most powerful and ancient spices, believed to aid digestion. It grows as an annual plant in the north of India and its leaves are used both fresh and dried. The dried seeds are small, hard, and yellowish, and have a pungent aroma—they are commonly used in ground spice mixes.

Flour
Indians use a variety of flours for cooking, the most common being wheat flour, which is used to make chapattis and other breads such as parathas, puris, and rotis. Chickpea flour, also known as gram flour or besan, is also used extensively. It is a dull yellow color, has an earthy aroma, and is much finer than wheat flour. Its rich, nutty taste is ideal for making light batters for fried snacks, such as pakoras and bhajias. It is also stirred into curries to thicken them. Water chestnut flour is often used in the preparation of snacks, particularly in Kashmir, where the singhara nut, a variety of water chestnut, is dried and ground to a flour.

Garam masala

Garam masala is a blend of spices—garam means "hot" or "aromatic" and masala means "mix". The spices and quantities used vary enormously from region to region and even from house to house—most cooks will boast their own very special blend, while keeping the exact ingredients a closely guarded secret. The spices can be ground coarsely or to a fine powder, which is usually sprinkled over a dish toward the end of the cooking time to release its aroma. There is no definitive recipe for garam masala, but see page 22 for my preferred recipe, as well as some regional variations.

Garlic (lahsun)

Garlic is a hardy, bulbous member of the onion family. The bulb consists of a number of cloves encased in a thin papery covering. It has a long history and is believed to have great curative powers, from aiding digestion to helping guard against infectious diseases. It has an unmistakable aroma and is eaten throughout India, except by some Kashmiri Hindus and the Jain sect. In Indian cooking it is most commonly used as a pulp and fried with ginger and onion in oil as a base in many recipes, particularly meat dishes. See page 18 for my tips on preparing garlic.

Ginger (adrak)

Ginger has a pungent, fresh aroma and has been prescribed for many ailments—a ginger infusion is great for a sore throat or cold, while I use it to cure travel sickness and nausea. It is the underground root, or rhizome, of a herbaceous plant grown throughout Asia. In its fresh state it is most often used as a pulp—the outer skin can be removed and the fibrous flesh is either finely chopped or pulped (see page 18) and used to impart a distinct flavor to a variety of dishes. Dried ginger is also available as a ground spice that can be used to flavor drinks, as well as savory and sweet dishes.

Gourd, bitter (karela)

The term gourd is applied loosely to some vegetables in the curcubit family, which encompasses pumpkins, both winter and summer squash, cucumbers, and melons. Bitter gourds or karela are native to India and have a green knobbly skin. I use them in spicy curries and dals (see page 90).

Gourd, bottle (doodhi)

Bottle gourd or doodhi is a wonderful vegetable that is great used in dals and spicy vegetable dishes (see page 108). It is long and marrow-shaped with a hard, pale green skin and sweet white flesh.

Jaggery (gur)

Jaggery is a dark, sticky, fudgelike sugar, which is made from sugar cane juice that has been boiled down. It has a distinct, musky flavor, and is used to sweeten a whole range of dishes. Brown sugar can be substituted, although it won't have quite the same sweet richness.

Lentils and legumes (dal)

The word "dal" means lentils or legumes and is often used to describe a lentil-based dish. Legumes are a good source of protein, and dal is a staple throughout India, particularly in the Punjab. There are many different varieties, but the most common ones are channa dal (white gram lentils), toover dal (yellow lentils), masoor dal (red lentils), and urad dal (black gram lentils). Dal is also used to describe chickpeas and red kidney beans.

Mango (aam)
Mangoes are widely cultivated throughout India and are used in cooking in both their ripe and unripe (green) states. Fresh mangoes are used in desserts and drinks and are rich in vitamin C. Mango chutneys and pickles are a firm favorite and are often highly spiced, while mango powder (amchoor) is dried ground mango that is used as a spice to give a sweet-and-sour flavor to snacks and lentil dishes.

Mint (pudhina)
This fresh herb is not used extensively in Indian cooking, but it does appear in recipes for chutneys and dips and in some specific meat and chicken dishes, such as Ground lamb with peas and mint (see page 68).

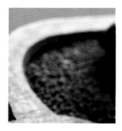

Mustard seeds (rai)
Round in shape and sharp tasting, mustard seeds are used to flavor a variety of dishes. Whole black mustard seeds are often thrown into hot oil or "popped" at the beginning of a recipe—this gives them a sweet, nutty taste that enhances vegetables, legumes, fish dishes, and relishes. The mustard plant is an annual that bears bright yellow flowers. The seeds of the plant, when dried, are the spice. There are three types of mustard seeds, of which brown and black are the most widely used in India.

Nutmeg and mace
(jaiphal/javitri)
Nutmeg and mace come from the same tree, mace being the lacy outer covering of the nutmeg kernel. Nutmeg has a warm, sweet flavor, and is used in small quantities in desserts, often grated from a whole nutmeg. It is also used in some garam masala mixes. Mace is similar in flavor, but is not as sweet and is more often used as a ground spice. Nutmeg is widely used in Indian medicine, and is believed to help overcome bronchitis and rheumatism.

Oil and ghee
Indians cook with a variety of oils. Peanut or sunflower oil is most commonly used for starting off dishes and is also used for deep-frying. Coconut oil, with its strong aroma, is used more in the south, while the dark yellow mustard oil is used extensively in Bengal in fish dishes. Ghee is clarified butter and many Indian recipes use ghee as the cooking fat. It can be heated to very high temperatures without burning and does not require refrigeration. In most cases oil can be substituted for ghee, and increasingly Indians are using the lighter vegetable oils as a healthier alternative.

Okra (bhendi)
Okra are the edible pods of an annual plant that grows in tropical and subtropical regions. The pods are typically ridged and contain small seeds and a sticky substance— however if you carefully wash and dry the okra before cooking you can prevent them going sticky. Okra is delicious when prepared as a dry vegetable dish (see page 88).

Paneer
Paneer is a fresh Indian cheese made with curdled milk, originally introduced by the Mughal invaders. It quickly became a favorite dish in the north, but it is now eaten all over India. It doesn't have a great deal of flavor, but it does have a wonderful firm texture and will take on other flavors during cooking. For vegetarians, it is also an excellent source of protein. It is often cubed and lightly fried until golden brown before being added to other ingredients. It holds its shape well and will not crumble during cooking. You can make your own, but good-quality paneer is much more readily available now so I would not recommend you go to the trouble of making it.

Pepper (kalamiri)

Pepper is the most commonly used spice and is sometimes known as the King of Spices. It is the fruit of a perennial vine which bears berries or peppercorns. The black, white, red, and green varieties all come from same plant—the difference in color occurs in the way they are processed. Black pepper is made by drying green peppercorns in the sun, while white pepper is made when ripe berries are softened in water, hulled, and then dried. In India, I used to pickle green peppercorns in brine—it's often used as a pickle in the winter months.

Poppy seeds (khus khus)

Indian poppy seeds are a pale ivory color and are used in cooking in a variety of ways—they can be ground with other spices to thicken sauces for meat and fish, and they are also used in sweet dishes and drinks. Poppy seeds come from the annual flowering plant, also known for its narcotic properties.

Rice

Rice is one of the main staples of Indian food, but is much more fundamental to the southern diet, whereas in northern India, bread is more commonly eaten as an accompaniment. In the south, you are likely to eat rice at every meal, from uttapam for breakfast to sweet rice puddings. Long-grain white rice is the most common, but there are countless varieties, from Kerala's red rice to the sticky rice of Assam. I always recommend using basmati rice as its aromatic flavor is far superior to other varieties.

Saffron (kesar)

Saffron is considered the most expensive spice in the world and is worth its weight in gold. It is actually made from the stigmas of the crocus flower, which are hand picked and dried in the sun. A gift of saffron is something very special and it is often exchanged at Diwali. Saffron, which is sold as strands and as a powder, is used in very small quantities to flavor both savory and sweet dishes.

Tamarind (imli)

The tamarind tree is evergreen and bears long, crescent-shaped pods. Within these pods are the seeds, surrounded by a fleshy pulp. It is this pulp, with its fruity sweet-and-sour aroma, that is used in Indian cooking. It appears in a number of south Indian and Gujarati lentil dishes and can be made into a wonderful sweet chutney (see page 111). According to Ayurvedic medicine, it is beneficial as a mild laxative, and tamarind water is often recommended to soothe a sore throat.

Turmeric (haldi)

Although used mainly for color, this spice imparts a subtle flavor and is also used extensively for its antiseptic and digestive properties. Turmeric is the root, or rhizome, of a herbaceous perennial plant related to the ginger family. This bright yellow, bitter-tasting spice is sold ground, although the small roots are also available fresh or dried. Like ginger, it needs to be peeled and ground before using. If your hands become stained when preparing fresh turmeric, you can clean them by rubbing them with potato peelings. Stains on work surfaces or dishes can be removed by covering them with baking soda and detergent. Leave for about 20 minutes and then rinse off.

My useful cooking tips

Cooking authentic Indian food can seem daunting to many cooks, but it doesn't have to be that way—trust me! When I first came to live in England, many of the herbs and spices and other specialist ingredients were difficult to find, but now they are readily available in good supermarkets and Asian grocers.

One of the things that I hear over and over is that the ingredients lists in Indian recipes are too long and many people think that this means that they have to spend a lot of time preparing ingredients. I've been cooking almost all my life, and with a family to feed (which often means extended family), I have learned a few tricks on saving time—without compromising on flavor. So, whether you are preparing ingredients in advance, storing spices and herbs, or making fresh pulps and pastes, follow my advice and you will soon find that you are cooking authentic Indian food without any hassle.

As you look through the recipes in this book you will see that some ingredients appear often and form the basis for many dishes. Garlic, ginger, onions, and cilantro are used extensively in Indian cooking, along with certain other spices and herbs. Buying and preparing these from scratch every time you want to cook an Indian dish can be time-consuming and laborious, so here are some ideas and tips to help you.

Garlic

A large number of my recipes call for garlic pulp. One large clove will make about 1/2 teaspoon of garlic pulp. You can prepare it in batches and keep it for later. Simply peel the garlic cloves and puree in a food processor or blender with a little water until you have a smooth pulp. This will keep in airtight containers in the refrigerator for up to 10 days and can be used as necessary. If you want to be really organized, you can freeze garlic pulp in ice cube trays kept specifically for this purpose. Once frozen, remove from the trays and store in the freezer in airtight containers.

Fresh gingerroot

Exactly the same principle applies to gingerroot pulp, which is also a basic ingredient in many of my recipes. Simply peel the tough outer skin with a small sharp knife and roughly chop the ginger into small pieces. Puree the pieces in a food processor or blender with a little water until you have a smooth consistency. Again, you can store this in the refrigerator in airtight containers or freeze like garlic. I never like to waste anything, however, so I usually leave my ginger unpeeled, as there is a lot of flavor in the skin. Wash the gingerroot well and soak it for a few minutes in warm water to remove any dirt in the crevices. When I do decide to peel it, I keep the peelings and add them to a cup of hot water for a soothing ginger infusion.

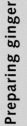
Preparing ginger

Onions

Onions are used in Indian cooking in many different ways—to flavor, color, thicken, or garnish dishes. If onions are being used to make a rich sauce for a meat dish they are usually fried slowly in oil or ghee. You can fry batches of sliced onions in advance and keep them in the refrigerator in airtight containers for up to two weeks. I use raw onions to season new cast-iron pans—simply cut an onion in half, wrap it in a piece of cheesecloth or similar thin cloth so you can hold it easily, dip into oil and then rub the cut side over the surface of a hot pan until it sizzles and starts to smell nicely of burned onion. Remove from the heat and wipe off the excess oil with a piece of kitchen towel.

Using and storing fresh herbs

The most commonly used fresh herb in Indian cooking is cilantro. It is used as a basis for green chutneys, as an ingredient in many vegetable and chicken dishes and, of course, as a fragrant and colorful garnish for a whole range of dishes. When chopped fresh cilantro is called for, most people usually just use the leaves, but I like to use the stems of the plant as well wherever I can—they are full of flavor and are great in soups and stocks. Fresh cilantro can quickly lose its flavor, but you can freeze it by washing the leaves well, leaving them to dry completely on a dish towel and then freezing in sealed plastic bags. They can then be used in cooking, although not as a garnish. Other fresh herbs, such as fenugreek leaves and curry leaves, can also be stored this way.

Many recipes, particularly those from southern India, call for fried curry leaves as a garnish. You can prepare these in advance: Simply fry them in hot oil for 2 to 3 minutes. Remove them from the pan with a slotted spoon, drain on paper towels, and, when cool, store in an airtight container for up to 10 days.

Spice pastes

Pastes form a very important part of Indian cooking. The one I have included here is a classic combination of flavors that is used to spice a number of dishes, especially vegetables, such as okra, eggplant and beans. One of my first memories is of watching our cook at home in India making this paste with a cylindrical crusher on a flat stone. He would place a clean cloth under this very heavy stone and sit with a bowl with all the ingredients mixed together. Working with a small amount at a time, he would crush the ingredients into a paste, occasionally sprinkling the stone with water. Most Indian households have their own basic masala and, once you understand the principle of blending ingredients together, you can play around with the ingredients to make your own version. Traditionally, this would be made fresh every day, but it will keep for five to six days if stored in a refrigerator.

Cilantro, chili, garlic, and ginger paste

(Makes about 12 tablespoons)

8 to 10 dried red chilies
6 cloves garlic, peeled
2-inch piece fresh gingerroot, chopped
2 large bunches fresh cilantro, stems and leaves, chopped
6 to 8 fresh curry leaves
1 tablespoon sea salt
2 tablespoons green chilies, chopped

The simplest way to make this paste is to place all the ingredients together in a food processor or blender and process to a smooth paste. Add 2 to 3 tablespoons of water as you blend to make a smooth consistency. Store in the refrigerator in an airtight container for up to six days.

Using and storing dried spices

Spices are an important part of Indian culture— and not just because they are used extensively in the cooking. Many of the spices that we use today have been part of Ayurvedic medicine for thousands of years and some are highly revered for their special powers (see pages 12 to 17 for more information on individual spices). However, it is food that we are concerned with here. If you are new to cooking Indian food you might find the range of spices daunting, but once you have grasped the basics of how spices work and what the most common flavor combinations are, you will soon be able to experiment and flavor your dishes to your own liking. An expert Indian cook knows instinctively how to mix and match certain flavors, when to add a little bit of something or other, and what is missing from a spice mixture. With my help you will begin to discover the secrets of using spices!

As you look through the recipes you will discover there is a certain order of cooking. There are spices that are always used at the beginning of a recipe, such as mustard seeds. These need to be "popped" in hot oil so the flavor can be

Opposite: Many Indian spices add color and texture, as well as flavor. From top: Whole dried red chilies, cumin seeds, ground turmeric, dried red chili flakes.

released. Cumin seeds are also often started off in this way. When they start to crackle you then add your "wet" ingredients, such as garlic, ginger, and onions. Ground spices are added after you have added the vegetables—they need to go in last otherwise they will burn and change the color and flavor of the dish. The spice mixture called garam masala is usually always added right at the end of a recipe—it does not need to be cooked for more than a few minutes, but will enhance the flavor of a finished dish.

Away with spice racks!

Spices really stay fresh for only about four weeks, although in hot weather some lose their flavor more quickly. Ground spices deteriorate even more quickly than whole ones because their essential oils evaporate more quickly. It is always better, if you can, to buy whole spices and then dry-roast and grind them as and when you need them. In some cases you can see when ground spices have turned stale—turmeric changes from bright to dull yellow, while ground red chilies lose their bright red color. One of the problems is that people don't realize that their wonderfully decorative spice racks are no good for storing spices, which begin to deteriorate as soon as they're exposed to light. The best way to store them is in airtight tins in a cupboard away from direct sunlight. Because I cook for my family every day, I grind up my spices in small quantities on a regular basis. I like to keep my spices in a spice box. In fact, I have two—one is for everyday flavors, such as coriander, cumin, turmeric, mustard seeds, and fenugreek, while the other is for aromatic spices, including mace, nutmeg, cinnamon, and green cardamom. Some spices, such as saffron and asafoetida should always be kept separate as they are very powerful. My advice is always to buy small quantities at a time. I also often leave my spices coarsely ground—the finer theyre ground the more quickly they lose their flavor.

My basic garam masala

Every household in India probably has its own special recipe for garam masala, handed down through the generations. In India, the basic mixture also varies from region to region. The spices in this mixture were traditionally those that heated the body and usually include cardamom, cloves, cinnamon, and nutmeg. Here is my recipe for garam masala, plus some regional variations. This quantity lasts me for about a month—you might prefer to make less if you are not cooking Indian food on a daily basis.

$1\frac{1}{2}$ ounces black cardamom pods

2 ounces green cardamom pods

2 whole nutmegs

2 bay leaves

20 x 1-inch pieces of cinnamon stick

10 tablespoons cumin seeds

8 tablespoons fennel seeds

5 tablespoons coriander seeds

2 teaspoons cloves

Dry-roast all the spices by putting them in a hot cast-iron skillet. Stir over medium heat for 3 minutes, or until the mixture starts smoking slightly. Remove from the heat and leave to cool on paper towels. Transfer to a coffee or spice grinder and process until you have a fine powder (although I prefer to leave my mixture very coarse). Store in a dry airtight container with a tight-fitting lid and keep out of direct sunlight. Use within one month.

South Indian garam masala

8 dried red chilies

$1\frac{1}{2}$ teaspoons fenugreek seeds

2 tablespoons coriander seeds

3 teaspoons cumin seeds

1 teaspoon black mustard seeds

15 curry leaves

$1\frac{1}{2}$ teaspoons black peppercorns

2 or 3 green cardamom pods

1 teaspoon ground ginger

1 tablespoon ground turmeric

Dry-roast and grind all the whole spices. Add the ground ginger and turmeric, cool, and store in an airtight container.

Preparing garam masala

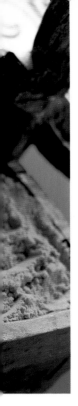

Left: **A spice box containing fenugreek seeds, dried red chili, mustard seeds, ground turmeric, and cumin seeds.**

East Indian garam masala
2 tablespoons fennel seeds
2 tablespoons cumin seeds
3 tablespoons black mustard seeds
1 tablespoon fenugreek seeds
1 tablespoon coriander seeds
3 or 4 cloves
1-inch piece of cinnamon stick
2 or 3 dried red chilies
pinch of asafoetida

Dry-roast and grind all the whole spices. Add the asafoetida and blend together briefly. Cool and store in an airtight container.

North Indian garam masala
3-inch piece of cinnamon stick
2 tablespoons cumin seeds
1 tablespoon coriander seeds
4 bay leaves
3 or 4 black cardamom pods
10 cloves
1 teaspoon black peppercorns
$1/2$ teaspoon ground mace
pinch of ground nutmeg
8 saffron strands

Dry-roast all the whole spices, except the saffron. Add the saffron strands, mace, and nutmeg, cool and store in an airtight container.

West Indian garam masala
3 tablespoons cumin seeds
4 dried red chilies
2 tablespoons sesame seeds
1 tablespoon fennel seeds
6 green cardamom pods
1 tablespoons ajowan seeds
1 tablespoon coriander seeds
pinch of asafoetida

Dry-roast the whole spices and grind. Add the asafoetida, cool and store in an airtight container.

My kitchen equipment

Indian cooking does not involve complicated cooking techniques, so you won't have to buy a lot of specialist equipment. However, these are some of the things I have to hand in my kitchen:

Karhai Also known as a kadai, this is the Indian version of the wok. Made of cast-iron, it is very versatile—you can use it for deep-frying, stir-frying, and steaming, or for simmering meat. It is ideal to have a ring on top of the burner so the pan sits steady on it and there is no danger of it tumbling over.

Pans and frying pans Heavy-bottomed pans are ideal as you will be able to cook over medium heat for longer periods without burning. Tight-fitting lids are also helpful as they stop steam from escaping. A good skillet, preferably cast-iron, is particularly useful for dry-frying spices before grinding, because this type of pan can be heated without any liquid.

Thali Traditionally, this is a large, stainless-steel plate used to serve a whole Indian meal on one plate (see page 93). The food, comprising several different dishes is served in small dishes (katoris). These can be lined around the edge of the plate, while in the middle there will be breads and rice, pickles, and poppadums.

Mortar and pestle I use a mortar and pestle for small quantities of whole spices, as well as for crushing garlic and ginger.

Grater A stainless-steel grater can come in handy to grate ginger, garlic, carrot, nutmeg, etc. An Indian grater is used horizontally over a bowl.

Coconut grater I love this piece of equipment— it makes preparing fresh coconut incredibly simple. It clamps to the countertop and is very useful if you use a lot of freshly grated coconut in cooking. Mine is plastic, but traditionally they were metal. You can use an ordinary grater (see page 111).

Tawa This is the traditional flat griddle used to make Indian breads, such as chapattis and parathas. Large, flat tawas are sometimes also used to make dosas (flat rice pancakes). Any flat griddle pan can be used as an alternative.

Blender and spice grinder In India, I watched spices being ground on an Indian grinding stone, but I find it much easier to use an electric blender for pureeing or blending drinks, soups, and sauces. A small spice grinder or coffee grinder is excellent for grinding dry spices.

Knives Since Indian cooking involves a lot of chopping, use good knives with firm handles and sharp steel blades. An all-purpose, medium-size cook's knife is essential. Sharpen your knives regularly with a steel sharpener.

Tongs A pair of long tongs are useful for turning chapattis on a hot griddle and can also be used for frying pappadums in oil and removing them for draining after.

Skewers When barbecuing meat, fish, or vegetables, thick metal skewers are useful as the food does not rotate on the skewer during cooking. Metal skewers do not burn when suspended over live coal and they can also be cleaned and re-used.

Rolling pin/chapatti board Traditional Indian rolling pins are longer and thinner than western ones; we use them to roll out flat breads on a special round chapatti board. However, a conventional rolling pin can also be used to roll out your chapattis on a clean, dry, well-floured countertop.

NOTE
- All recipes serve 4 unless otherwise stated.
- All eggs are large
- Flours are measured by scooping with the measuring cup and leveling the surface.

1 teaspoon = 5 ml
1 tablespoon = 15 ml

Appetizers, snacks, and soups

Indians love to snack. Whatever the time of day you will find little food stalls luring passersby with all manner of street food. Eating on the hoof is second nature in India, and many Indian people just can't resist the temptations of the food stalls, which serve hot, freshly made samosas, pooris, and bhajias, to name a few. The snacks in this chapter are sold as street food, but they would still be made in the home as well, and many of them I learned at a very young age by watching my grandmother. As entertaining in the home is a very important part of Indian culture, we would often prepare snack items to offer guests who dropped by—who would almost certainly take up the offer. Soups are really only drunk in the north of India, and it is only recently that they have begun to be served as a course. They were more usually drunk instead of tea—often in colder climates where you would do what you could to keep warm—and what better way to lift your spirits than to cup your hands around a warming bowl of soup!

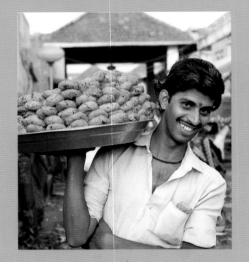

Above: **Fast food vendors in the Koyambedu wholesale fruit and vegetable market in Chennai.** *Opposite:* **A roadside stall in Kerala serves spicy chickpeas with spinach to hungry passersby.**

Samosas

Spicy potato and green pea filled pastries

These tasty snacks are served all over India, from Mumbai to Rajasthan. The fillings vary enormously from region to region. In the south, where the population is more Muslim, beef or lamb fillings can be found. For Diwali, samosas are made with sweet fillings. The farther north you go, the more pyramid-shaped the samosas tend to become.

Makes 16

1³/₄ cups peeled potatoes, cut into small chunks
²/₃ cup shelled peas
3 tablespoons oil or ghee
1¹/₂ teaspoons coriander seeds, crushed
1 tablepsoon chopped fresh gingerroot
5 cloves garlic, chopped
1 green chili, chopped
2 teaspoons ground coriander
³/₄ teaspoon ground cumin
¹/₂ teaspoon ground fennel
pinch of salt
4 tablespoons chopped fresh cilantro
16 sheets phyllo pastry dough, each 3 x 8 inches
    (see My tip)
all-purpose flour and water for sealing
vegetable oil for deep-frying

Bring a large pan of salted water to a boil. Add the potatoes to the pan and cook for 15 to 20 minutes until soft; drain and leave to cool.

Cook the peas in boiling water for 5 minutes; drain and set aside. Roughly mash the potatoes and mix with the peas.

Heat the oil or ghee in a large pan and add the crushed coriander seeds. When they begin to crackle, add the ginger, garlic, and green chili. Fry for 2 minutes. Add the ground spices, sprinkle with water, and fry for 3 to 4 minutes over low heat. Pour the mixture over the potatoes and peas and mix well. Add the salt and chopped fresh cilantro.

Use one rectangle of phyllo pastry dough. Place 1 teaspoon of filling on the top corner. Make the first diagonal fold, then the second and the third (see opposite).

Open up the pouch and spoon in a little more filling, taking care not to overfill, or it will burst while being fried. Make a paste with flour and water and smear on the remaining flap. Close and press to "glue" the opening and seal the filling in the samosa.

Deep-fry a few samosas at a time in hot oil at 375°F for 5 to 10 minutes. Remove from the oil with a slotted spoon and leave to drain on paper towels. Serve warm with Cilantro and mint raita or Tamarind and date chutney (see page 110).

◇ **My tip** I use phyllo pastry dough because it's easy to use, it's light, and doesn't soak up so much oil. Keep the phyllo pastry sheets covered with a damp cloth while you are working to prevent them drying out.

Preparing samosas

◆ **My tip** If you have any scraps of phyllo pastry dough left over, you can cut them into small pieces and deep-fry in hot oil. They are delicious served with Nimboo ka phool, a zesty, dry dip made from salt, ground red chilies, black pepper, sugar, and a pinch of citric acid powder.

Khaman dhokla
Steamed chickpea flour pancakes

These pancakes from Gujarat are served as part of a main meal and would most usually be eaten at weekends for brunch. They are very filling, but absolutely delicious.

Serves 4
2 cups chickpea flour
1/2 cup plain yogurt
1/2 teaspoon baking soda
1/2 teaspoon ground turmeric
1 green chili, chopped
1-inch piece fresh gingerroot, chopped
salt, to taste
juice of 1/2 lemon
2 tablespoons vegetable oil
1/2 teaspoon mustard seeds
2 tablespoons chopped fresh cilantro
2 tablespoons grated fresh coconut

Mix the chickpea flour with the yogurt and enough warm water to form a thick batter. Mix in the baking soda and ground turmeric and leave to ferment for about 1 hour in a warm place.

Using a mortar and pestle, crush the green chili and ginger to a fine paste, then add to the chickpea flour and yogurt mixture. Add the salt and lemon juice and mix well.

Grease a shallow cake pan. Pour the batter into the mold and bake at 375°F for 10 to 15 minutes. The batter will have risen to about 1 1/2 inches. Leave to cool and cut into 1 1/2-inch squares. Arrange on a serving dish.

Heat the oil in a small pan and add the mustard seeds. When they begin to crackle, pour over the cooked dhoklas.

Serve garnished with chopped cilantro and grated coconut.

Pakoras
Vegetable fritters

These are a favorite snack all over India. Chickpea flour is most commonly used for the batter and really gives the best crispness, although you could use all-purpose flour or a mixture of all-purpose flour and rice flour.

Serves 4
200 g (7 oz) chickpea flour
1/2 teaspoon ground turmeric
pinch of asafoetida
salt, to taste
vegetable oil for deep-frying
2 onions, peeled and cut into 1-inch dice
2 red bell peppers, cut into 1-inch dice
2 green bell peppers, cut into 1-inch dice
12 spinach leaves, washed
2 potatoes, peeled and cut into thin slices

Mix together the chickpea flour, ground turmeric, asafoetida, and salt. Add 1 1/4 cups water, a little at a time, and mix to make a thick, smooth batter.

Heat the oil in a deep-fryer or large, heavy-bottomed saucepan to 375°F. Dip each piece of vegetable into the batter to coat completely.

Fry in the hot oil, one or two pieces at a time, until they turn golden brown, about 5 minutes. Remove from the oil with a slotted spoon and drain on paper towels.

Serve immediately with tomato ketchup or Cilantro and mint raita (see page 110).

Opposite: **Vegetable fritters**

Pyaaz ke bhajie
Onion bhajias

These delicious, light, crisp snacks are immensely popular all over India and are a far cry from the heavy, stodgy versions found in many Indian restaurants. If I ever have any left over (and this would be a rarity in my family), I love them roughly chopped and added to a fresh crunchy salad.

Serves 4 to 6
2¹/₄ cups chickpea flour
1 teaspoon garlic pulp
¹/₂ teaspoon ground turmeric
³/₄ teaspoon cayenne pepper
salt, to taste
¹/₄ teaspoon asafoetida
2³/₄ cups sliced onions
2 tablespoons chopped fresh cilantro
vegetable oil for deep-frying

Mix together the chickpea flour, 4 to 6 tablespoons water, garlic, ground turmeric, cayenne pepper, salt, and asafoetida to form a thick paste.

   Add the sliced onions and chopped cilantro. Make small dumplings and deep-fry in batches in hot oil, 375°F, for 10 to 15 minutes until they turn golden brown and the dumplings are cooked through. Remove with a slotted spoon and drain on paper towels.

Batata vada

Spiced potato dumplings

Batata vada is traditionally street food, although it can also be served as an accompaniment to a main meal. This is a very simple recipe and is a real favorite all over India. I've used ghee here for an extra buttery flavor.

Serves 4

3 large potatoes, peeled, boiled, and mashed
3/4 teaspoon salt
1/4 teaspoon coarsely ground black pepper
2 green chilies, finely chopped
heaping 1/3 cup water chestnut flour or cornstarch
1 tablespoon chopped fresh cilantro
1 teaspoon lemon juice
4 tablespoons ghee for shallow frying

Place all the ingredients, except the ghee, in a large bowl and mix well. Knead and make into small balls and then flatten into disks.

Heat the ghee in a shallow skillet. Fry the potato disks on both sides for 2 to 4 minutes, or until they turn crisp and golden. Drain on paper towels and serve hot or cold with a dip or raita.

◇ **My tip** If you can't get hold of water chestnut flour soak 2 slices of bread in 1/4 cup of water. Mash, press the excess moisture out, and add to the remainder of the ingredients. You might have to tweak the spicing up to obtain the desired flavor.

Khandvi

Chickpea flour pancake rolls

This is a Gujarati dish that I would normally serve as part of a main meal. Ideal dishes to go with it are Yogurt and spinach soup (see page 42), Princess salad (see page 109), Cauliflower with fresh cilantro and tomato (see page 85), and, of course, breads and samosas.

Serves 4

1-inch piece fresh gingerroot, chopped
1 green chili, chopped
1/2 cup plain yogurt
1/2 teaspoon ground turmeric
salt, to taste
1 cup plus 2 tablespoons chickpea flour, sifted
juice of 1/2 lemon
4 tablespoons vegetable oil
1/2 teaspoon mustard seeds
pinch of asafoetida
2 tablespoons grated fresh coconut
2 tablespoons chopped fresh cilantro

Crush the ginger and green chilies to a fine a paste using a mortar and pestle.

Grease a large metal baking sheet.

In a large pan, mix together the yogurt, 7 tablespoons water, turmeric, salt, and ginger and green chili paste. Stir in the chickpea flour and lemon juice, making sure there are not any lumps.

Place the pan over medium heat, stirring constantly to make a thick batter.

Quickly spread the mixture over the greased metal surface as thinly as possible while the batter is still hot.

Leave to cool for 2 to 3 minutes, then roll up from one edge to the other to form a layered cylindrical shape. Cut into 1-inch pieces and place on a serving dish.

Heat the oil and add the mustard seeds. When they begin to crackle, add the asafoetida, then pour over the pieces. Serve garnished with grated coconut and chopped cilantro.

Poricha yera
Spiced fried shrimp

This is very spicy, but is wonderful as an appetizer. If you wish to serve it as a main dish, the quantities shown here will serve 2 to 3 people. I serve it with yogurt or raita, bread, and greens.

Serves 4 to 6
2¼ pounds large raw shrimp, shelled and deveined with tails left on
salt, to taste
1 tablespoon lemon juice
1 teaspoon garlic pulp
¾ teaspoon ground turmeric
2½ teaspoons cayenne pepper
½ teaspoon ground fennel
2½ teaspoons ground cumin
1 egg yolk
vegetable oil for deep-frying
lemon wedges, to garnish

Sprinkle the shrimp with a pinch of salt and 1 teaspoon of lemon juice, set aside.

Mix together the remaining lemon juice, garlic pulp, turmeric, cayenne, ground fennel, ground cumin, egg yolk, and salt. Marinate the shrimp in the mixture and leave for 20 minutes.

Heat the oil to 375°F and then deep-fry the shrimp for 5 to 10 minutes until cooked. Serve hot with lemon wedges to garnish.

Ajwaini jheenga
Ajowan shrimp

This dish comes from Hyderabad, where ajowan seeds are used a lot with fish. I would serve this with a paratha or rice, vegetables, and a raita.

Serves 4
1 lemon
1 pound large raw shrimp, shelled and deveined
1 cup plain yogurt
4 teaspoons garlic pulp
½ teaspoon ground turmeric
1 teaspoon garam masala
2 teaspoons ajowan seeds
salt, to taste
2 tablespoons oil
1 tablespoon chopped fresh cilantro

Squeeze the juice of half the lemon over the shrimp; mix well and set aside. Mix the yogurt with all the remaining ingredients, except the oil and cilantro. Add the shrimp to the marinade and refrigerate for 2 to 3 hours.

Skewer the shrimp and cook over charcoal or under a broiler on a greased tray for a few minutes, turning once. Serve hot with the remaining lemon squeezed over and garnished with chopped cilantro.

Opposite: **Spiced fried shrimp**

Chili shrimp salad

On my travels throughout India, I am always fascinated by the variety of ingredients used for salads. This is a spicy salad from southeast Bengal, where it is served cold. If there is any left over, it is absolutely delicious on toast, or you can try serving it in vol-au-vent cases as a canapé.

Serves 4

2 tablespoons vegetable oil
11 ounces large raw shrimp, shelled and deveined
1 tablespoon tomato paste
1 cup chopped onions
1 cup chopped green bell peppers
1 tablespoon lemon juice
2 tomatoes, chopped
1 green chili, chopped
2 tablespoons chopped fresh cilantro
2 tablespoons mango pickle
3 tablespoons mustard oil (see My tip)
salt, to taste
1 teaspoon sugar
chopped fresh cilantro, to garnish

Heat the vegetable oil in a skillet or karhai. Add the shrimp and stir-fry for 3 to 4 minutes over medium heat.

Stir in the tomato paste then remove from the heat and put into a bowl large enough for the other ingredients to be mixed in later. Leave to cool for 30 to 45 minutes.

Mix in the remaining ingredients and serve sprinkled with chopped cilantro.

◈ **My tip** Mustard oil is often used in Indian cooking—it has a rich, nutty flavor that I love. I also like to use the oil from a jar of mango pickle—it is wonderful for adding flavor, as all the spice flavors from the pickle will have been absorbed by the oil.

Tandoori macchi

Fish kabobs

These delicious fish kabobs are best cooked over charcoal, although you can cook them under a broiler or on a gas barbecue. The ajowan seeds have excellent digestive properties, and are used extensively in barbecued fish recipes. Serve with bread and raita, a vegetable dish, or a dal.

Serves 4
juice of ½ lime
14 ounces cod or haddock, skinned cut into 2-inch cubes
chopped fresh cilantro, to garnish

For the marinade:
1 cup thick plain yogurt
1 tablespoon garlic pulp
2 teaspoons ginger pulp
1 tablespoon salt
1 teaspoon garam masala
1 teaspoon ajowan seeds
1 tablespoon vegetable oil

Make the marinade by mixing together the yogurt, garlic, ginger, salt, and garam masala in a bowl. Sprinkle the ajowan seeds over and pour the oil over the surface of the yogurt mixture.

Squeeze the lime juice over the pieces of fish and then immerse them in the yogurt marinade. Place in the refrigerator for at least 2 hours.

When you are ready to barbecue, thread the pieces of fish onto skewers.

Cook suspended over the heat for about 15 minutes: Make sure the pieces of fish do not touch any of the coals or the wire mesh. Turn frequently and baste with a little oil.

Serve garnished with chopped cilantro.

Hariyali tikka

Green chicken kabobs

Hariyali means "green" and this dish gets its name from the spinach and lovely fresh green herbs used in the marinade. It is great as an appetizer but can also be served as a main course with a dal, rice, and some bread. A similar dish is made in the southern states of Hyderabad. I love this served with Lentils with cream and butter (see page 106) or a buttery paratha (see page 99).

Serves 4
5 ounces fresh spinach leaves
1 ounce fresh mint
1 ounce fresh cilantro
1 green chili
1 cup plain yogurt
1 tablespoon garlic pulp
1 egg yolk
1 teaspoon garam masala
salt, to taste
1 pound chicken breast meat, skinned and cut into 1- to 1½-inch cubes

Bring a large pan of salted water to a boil and blanch the spinach leaves quickly; drain and refresh by plunging in cold water. Drain again and place in a food processor or blender with the mint, cilantro, and green chili. Process to a fine paste and set aside.

Mix the yogurt with the garlic pulp, egg yolk, garam masala, and the green paste. Mix well and add the salt. Add the chicken pieces, cover, and refrigerate for 4 to 5 hours.

The chicken can either be skewered and cooked over charcoal or arranged on a greased tray and broiled or baked in the oven. These kabobs will take about 10 minutes to cook.

Opposite: **Fish kabobs and Green chicken kabobs**

Elaichi malai tikka

Cardamom-flavored chicken

This delicately scented dish comes from the Muslim state of Hyderabad, where almonds and nuts are used a lot in the cooking. Elaichi means "cardamom", malai means "cream" and "tikka" refers to the fact that the chicken is in bite-size pieces.

Serves 4

1¹/₄ pounds chicken breast meat, skinned and cut
    into 1- to 1¹/₂ -inch cubes
juice of 1 lemon
1 cup plain yogurt
2 tablespoons garlic pulp
1 teaspoon ground cardamom
¹/₄ cup light cream
1 egg yolk
¹/₄ cup finely ground blanched almonds
salt, to taste
¹/₂ teaspoon garam masala
2 tablespoons chopped fresh cilantro
vegetable oil for greasing
thinly sliced onions and chopped fresh cilantro,
    to garnish

Wash and pat dry the chicken and then squeeze the lemon juice over. Rub into the chicken and set aside.

Mix the yogurt with all the remaining ingredients, except the oil, and beat well. Add the chicken pieces and refrigerate to marinate for 5 to 6 hours.

The chicken can be either skewered and cooked over charcoal or arranged on a greased tray and broiled or cooked inside the oven. Cook for 10 to 15 minutes.

Serve with an accompaniment of fresh onion rings and chopped fresh cilantro to garnish.

Seekh kebab

Ground lamb kabob

There are lots of versions of this dish, but this is the one I make at home for my family. The papaya tenderizes the meat. Ground coriander can be used instead of turmeric, or you can leave out the garlic and add more ginger. A good way of serving these kabobs is in a chapatti wrap with a yogurt raita and fresh cilantro, accompanied by thinly sliced onions and a tomato salad.

Serves 4

1 pound ground lamb
1 cup sliced onions
1 tablespoon garlic pulp
4 teaspoons ginger pulp
3 tablespoons chopped fresh mint
3 tablespoons chopped fresh cilantro
3/4 teaspoon cayenne pepper
1/2 teaspoon ground turmeric
1 teaspoon garam masala
1 ounce fresh papaya
salt, to taste
4 tablespoons (1/2 stick) butter, melted

Mix all the ingredients together, except the butter. Place in a food processor or blender and process until you have a coarse paste. Mix in half the melted butter.

Take a handful of the mixture and wrap it around a skewer to form a sausage shape about 4 inches long and 1 inch thick. Roll in your hands to make sure the meat is firmly compressed around the skewer. Repeat with the remaining mixture to make 8 kabobs.

Cook over charcoal or under a hot broiler for about 10 minutes. Remove from the skewer and smear with the remaining melted butter or oil and serve hot.

◇ **Note** The kabobs can be cooked under the broiler or on a gas barbecue, but the traditional flavor from the charcoal will be lost.

Left: **Ground lamb kabob**

Dahi palak shorbha
Yogurt and spinach soup

In winter, I always used to look forward to coming home from school as I would be handed a big cup of this nutritious soup and some spiced potato wedges.

Serves 4

2¹/₂ tablespoons chickpea flour
2¹/₂ cups water
5 ounces fresh spinach, shredded
1 cup plain yogurt
1-inch piece fresh gingerroot, finely chopped
2 small green chilies, finely chopped
¹/₂ teaspoon sugar
salt, to taste
1 tablespoon chopped fresh cilantro

Place the chickpea flour in a large bowl with 7 tablespoons of the water; stir together and set aside.

Blanch the shredded spinach in boiling water; drain, refresh in cold water, and drain again.

In a large bowl, mix the remaining water with the yogurt, chopped ginger, green chilies, and sugar. Add salt and beat well. Add the chickpea flour mixture to the above and place over medium heat, whisking frequently.

When the mixture begins to boil, reduce the heat to a simmer and add the blanched spinach.

Increase the heat to boiling point and serve piping hot, garnished with cilantro.

Khumbh ka shorbha
Kashmiri mushroom soup

In India, fresh morels would be used for this recipe—they have a rich, earthy flavor. When I make this at home I sometimes use a mixture of fresh mushrooms and dried morels.

Serves 4

3 tablespoons vegetable oil
1 cup chopped onions
1 tablespoon garlic pulp
4 teaspoons ginger pulp
2¹/₄ pounds button mushrooms, chopped
¹/₂ teaspoon ground turmeric
³/₄ teaspoon cayenne pepper
2 teaspoons garam masala
1 cup chopped tomatoes
2¹/₂ cups water
4 tablespoons (¹/₂ stick) butter
¹/₃ cup all-purpose flour
2 teaspoons sugar
salt, to taste
juice of ¹/₂ lemon
chopped fresh cilantro, to garnish

Heat the oil in a large pan. Add the onions and fry for 2 to 3 minutes.

Add the garlic, ginger, mushrooms, turmeric, cayenne, and garam masala and cook, stirring constantly, for 5 to 8 minutes. Add the chopped tomatoes and water and bring to a boil. Simmer for about 20 minutes and then set aside. When it has cooled slightly, place in a food processor or blender and process until smooth. Strain the mixture into another pan and heat.

Mix together the butter and flour. Use lumps of this to thicken the simmering soup, stirring in a piece at a time. Add the sugar, salt, and lemon juice.

Serve the soup hot sprinkled with chopped fresh cilantro.

Tamatar shorbha

Tomato soup

This is another recipe from the north of India. This Indian version of a classic favorite is deliciously aromatic and will warm the soul.

Serves 6 to 8

2¼ pounds tomatoes, chopped
1 quart tomato juice
5 teaspoons ginger pulp
1 tablespoon garlic pulp
8 to 10 cardamom pods
1 teaspoon ground paprika
½ teaspoon ground turmeric
1 quart water
½ cup all-purpose flour
6 tablespoons (¾ stick) butter
4 teaspoons sugar
salt, to taste
2 tablespoons vegetable oil
1 teaspoon ajowan seeds
2 cloves garlic, chopped
light cream, to garnish
1 tablespoon chopped fresh cilantro

Place the chopped tomatoes, tomato juice, ginger, garlic, cardamom pods, paprika, turmeric, and water in a large pan and bring to a boil. Cover and simmer for about 1 hour.

In a bowl mix the flour with the butter and add to the tomato mixture. Stir well and cook, stirring, for another 2 minutes. Strain the mixture into another pan and heat. Add the sugar and salt.

In another pan, heat the oil. Add the ajowan seeds and chopped garlic and cook, stirring, until the garlic turns golden brown. Stir into the soup and serve immediately, garnished with cream and chopped cilantro.

◇ **My tip** Sometimes if I really feel like cheating I buy a large can of tomato soup, water it down a little, and then add all my own spices and a few chopped fresh tomatoes.

Gajjar ka shorbha

Carrot and cilantro soup

Carrot and cilantro soup has become something of a classic—the pungent, slightly citrus flavor of cilantro complements the sweet flavor of carrots perfectly. This Indian version is spicier and has more of a kick.

Serves 4

1³/₄ cups carrots, roughly chopped

³/₄ cup sliced onions

1 tablespoon ginger pulp

1 tablespoon garlic pulp

1 quart water

2 teaspoons ground coriander

³/₄ teaspoon cayenne pepper

¹/₂ teaspoon ground turmeric

1 teaspoon ground fennel

¹/₂ teaspoon ground cumin

1 cup chopped tomatoes

2 tablespoons vegetable oil

2 tablespoons chickpea flour

1 teaspoon sugar

juice of ¹/₂ lemon

2 tablespoons chopped fresh cilantro

salt, to taste

Place the carrots in a pan with the sliced onions, ginger, garlic, and water. Add all the ground spices, stir together, and bring to a boil. Lower the heat and simmer for about 1 hour, or until the carrots become very soft.

Remove from the heat and add the tomatoes. Leave to cool and then process in a food processor or blender, or pass through a strainer, strain the liquid and set aside.

Heat the oil in another pan and over medium heat. Add the chickpea flour and cook for 2 to 3 minutes, stirring to make a paste. Pour in the carrot stock, a little at a time, whisking well to avoid any lumps forming until all the stock is used up.

Increase the heat and cook for about 5 minutes. Add the sugar, lemon juice, and half of the cilantro. Season and serve garnished with the chopped cilantro.

Mattar aur hare pyaaz ka shorbha

Green pea and scallion soup

This lovely, fresh soup is best made with fresh shelled peas, but if they are not in season, use frozen peas.

Serves 4

2 tablespoons vegetable oil

³/₄ cup sliced onions

1 tablespoon garlic pulp

4 teaspoons ginger pulp

2 cups shelled peas

¹/₂ teaspoon ground turmeric

¹/₂ teaspoon ground cumin

1¹/₂ quarts water

2 teaspoons garam masala

2 tablespoons chopped fresh mint

juice of ¹/₂ lemon

salt, to taste

1¹/₂ tablespoons cornstarch

¹/₄ cup scallions, sliced in small rounds

2 tablespoons chopped fresh cilantro, to garnish

Heat the oil in a large, heavy-bottomed pan and fry the onions, garlic, and ginger for 2 minutes. Add the peas and cook, stirring, for about 5 minutes. Add the ground turmeric and cumin.

Add the water, and bring to a boil. Simmer for about 25 minutes. Remove from the heat, leave to cool and then place the mixture in a food processor or blender. Process to a fine puree and then pass through a strainer. Add the garam masala, chopped mint, lemon juice, and salt.

In a small bowl, mix the cornstarch with a little water until you have a thin liquid the same consistency as cream. Bring the soup to a boil again and thicken with the cornstarch mixture, whisking in a little at a time.

Sprinkle the scallions over the soup with the chopped cilantro.

Handmade pappadums

Jehangiri shorbha
Spicy chicken soup

Another warming north Indian dish, this is acutally more of a broth than a soup. If you can't get hold of chicken bones, use 1¹/² quarts chicken stock instead.

Serves 6 to 8

4¹/² pounds raw chicken bones

1¹/⁴ pounds onions, sliced

1 tablespoon garlic pulp

4 teaspoons ginger pulp

³/⁴ teaspoon ground turmeric

1 tablespoon ground coriander

1 teaspoon ground fennel

1¹/² teaspoons ground cumin

8 cardamom pods

5 bay leaves

8 cloves

1 can (14-oz) crushed tomatoes

3 ounces fresh cilantro

2 ounces fresh mint

¹/⁴ cup vegetable oil

¹/² cup plus 1 tablespoon chickpea flour

¹/² teaspoon salt

juice of ¹/² lemon

chopped mint leaves and finely diced poached
    chicken, to garnish

First make the stock. Place the chicken bones in a large, heavy-bottomed saucepan and cover with cold water. Add all the ingredients, except the oil, chickpea flour, salt, lemon juice, and mint leaves and bring to a boil. Simmer for 3 to 4 hours until the water is reduced to one-third of its original quantity. Strain the stock through a fine strainer or cheesecloth and put into another pan to boil.

In a separate pan, combine the oil and chickpea flour and cook, stirring, for 2 to 3 minutes over low heat. When the chickpea flour begins to bubble, add the mixture to the strained chicken stock and bring to a boil, making sure no lumps form and the stock becomes slightly thicker in consistency.

Add the salt and lemon juice. Serve garnished with diced chicken and mint.

Left: A pappadum factory in Chennai. Pappadums are one of the most popular snacks in India and are eaten with most main meals. They are made from a split-pea dough, which is left plain or flavored with black pepper, chilies, or garlic. They are then shaped by hand into small, round patties, rolled into thin disks, and then left to dry in the sun.

Fish and shellfish

India's coastline stretches for almost 10,000 miles, so it's not surprising that fishing is a major industry. Fresh fish is now available in most of the big cities of India, many of which are miles from the sea, although it holds a particularly special place in the cuisine of the coastal regions.

In southern India, coconut palms line the beaches so, for example, Kerala has become famous for its fish curries, delicately scented with coconut. To the north, Mumbai and Calcutta all have their own special dishes, depending on what else is grown in the region and what the historical influences have been. The Parsis, who settled on the west coast, like their food sweet and sour, so dishes from Mumbai often use a lot of jaggery and tamarind, whereas Bengalis love to flavor fish with a pungent mustard-seed paste. Some of the varieties of fish used in Indian cooking are different from those used in cooler climes, but shellfish such as shrimp and lobster are very popular. Pomfret is probably my favorite fish. This nicely shaped flat fish is perfect for shallow-frying, broiling, roasting, or steaming in banana leaves. It is available from good fish merchants (often in frozen form from overseas), but you can substitute other firm white fish such as monkfish, sea bass, or swordfish.

Above: **A basket of fish, fresh out of the sea, and a local fishing boat on the beach at Chennai.** *Opposite:* **Selecting fresh shrimp at a seafood stall right by the sea in Cochin.**

Jheenga curry

Goan shrimp curry

This is a very simple, easy recipe of which there are many different versions. This is my favorite one—I love to eat this curry with just plain rice.

Serves 4
4 tablespoons vegetable oil
1 cup sliced onions
3 green chilies, sliced
7 tablespoons coconut milk
12 ounces large shelled raw shrimp
1 tablespoon tamarind pulp
salt, to taste

For the paste:
1 cup shredded coconut
8 whole dried red chilies
4 teaspoons coriander seeds
2¹/₂ teaspoons cumin seeds
¹/₂ teaspoon ground turmeric
1 teaspoon ginger pulp
1 teaspoon garlic pulp
2 teaspoons black peppercorns

Place all the ingredients for the paste in a food processor or blender and process until you have a fine paste, adding a little water as necessary.

Heat the oil in a wok or karhai and sauté the onions until golden brown. Add the ground paste mixture and cook, stirring, for 2 minutes.

Add the sliced green chilies and a little water to thin the paste to a sauce consistency. Add the coconut milk and raw shrimp and simmer for 5 minutes.

Add the tamarind pulp and salt. Cook for 2 minutes longer. Serve with plain rice.

Karhai jheenga

Shrimp in a spicy tomato sauce

This is now eaten more in northern India, although it originated on the east coast. It takes its name from the karhai, the round-bottomed, cast-iron pan in which it is cooked.

Serves 4
2 tablespoons vegetable oil
1 teaspoon cumin seeds
1¹/₂ cups diced onions
1 tablespoon garlic pulp
1 tablespoon ginger pulp
2 cups chopped tomatoes
¹/₂ teaspoon ground turmeric
¹/₂ teaspoon cayenne pepper
14 ounces large raw shrimp, shelled and deveined
salt, to taste
pinch of sugar
¹/₂ teaspoon crushed black peppercorns
1 teaspoon crushed coriander seeds
1 teaspoon ground fennel
¹/₂ teaspoon dried red chili flakes
3 tablespoons chopped fresh cilantro, to garnish

Heat the oil. Add the cumin seeds and when they begin to crackle add the diced onions and fry for 10 minutes. Add the garlic and ginger and fry for another minute. Stir in the chopped tomatoes, turmeric, and cayenne.

Sauté and cook for 10 minutes, stirring constantly. Sprinkle with a little water, if needed.

When the oil begins to separate, add the shrimp, salt to taste, and sugar and cook for 8 to 10 minutes.

Add the crushed black pepper, coriander seeds, ground fennel, and crushed red chilies. Cook for 1 minute longer and add half of the chopped cilantro.

Sprinkle with the remaining cilantro and serve with rice or parathas.

Opposite: **Shrimp in a spicy tomato sauce**

Chingri malai curry

Shrimp in a coconut cream sauce

This is a dish from the east coast of India. I always use fresh shrimp but frozen shrimp will also work well.

Serves 4

2½ cups chopped onions

4 cloves garlic

1 teaspoon ginger pulp

2¼ pounds large raw shrimp, shelled and deveined

salt, to taste

¾ teaspoon ground turmeric

4 tablespoons mustard or vegetable oil

4 cloves

4 green cardamom pods

1-inch piece of cinnamon stick

2 bay leaves

¾ teaspoon cayenne pepper

¼ cup plain yogurt

1½ cups coconut milk

Place the onions, garlic, and ginger in a food processor or blender and process to a fine paste.

Smear the shrimp with a little salt and half the turmeric. Heat 1 tablespoon of the oil in a skillet or karhai and fry the shrimp over high heat until just golden brown; remove and set aside.

Add the remaining oil to the pan. Add the cloves, cardamom, cinnamon, and bay leaves, reduce the heat, and add the onion, garlic, and ginger paste to the pan. Stir-fry over medium heat for 2 minutes.

Add the remaining turmeric and cayenne. Sprinkle with a little water and stir well. Add the yogurt and mix well. Pour in the coconut milk and return the shrimp to the pan. Cook over medium heat for 5 to 8 minutes until the shrimp are cooked and the sauce thickens.

Serve with plain boiled rice.

Jheenga patio

Shrimp with coconut and cashew nuts

Patio is a very typical Parsi dish from the west coast of India. The Parsis settled there after fleeing from Iran in the seventh century. Their food is typically sweet and sour, which is why ingredients such as jaggery and tamarind feature in their dishes.

Serves 4

⅔ cup unsalted cashew nuts

½ cup poppy seeds

2 cups grated fresh coconut

1 ounce tamarind pulp

4 tablespoons vegetable oil

3 teaspoons garlic pulp

1 teaspoon cumin seeds

10 to 12 curry leaves

½ teaspoon ground turmeric

1 teaspoon cayenne pepper

1 ounce jaggery or 2 tablespoons brown sugar

salt, to taste

14 ounces large raw shrimp, shelled and deveined

Soak the cashew nuts and poppy seeds in water for a few hours and then drain. Grind to a fine paste using a mortar and pestle with the grated coconut and tamarind pulp, adding a little water if needed; set aside.

Heat the oil in a karhai, wok, or large skillet, add the garlic pulp and stir-fry for a few minutes until brown. Add the cumin seeds and curry leaves. After a minute, add the turmeric, cayenne, and jaggery. Stir-fry for a couple of minutes.

Add the coconut-and-cashew nut paste to the pan and stir quickly, adding a little water to make the sauce thinner. Bring to a boil and then add the shrimp. Cook, stirring, for about 10 minutes, or until the shrimp are cooked.

Serve with a dal, rice, Mixed vegetable raita (see page 111), or Vegetable biryani (see page 84).

Left: **Shrimp in a coconut cream sauce**

Poricha meen
Broiled fish fillets

This dish comes from the coastal region on the southernmost tip of India. I generally use pomfret, but you could use other firm-fleshed fish, such as thick salmon or swordfish steaks or halibut or cod fillets.

Serves 4
1¹⁄₂ pounds thick fish steaks (or thick skinless fillets), such as pomfret, halibut, salmon, or swordfish
1 teaspoon garlic pulp
1 teaspoon cayenne pepper
¹⁄₂ teaspoon ground turmeric
salt, to taste
2 tablespoons lemon juice

Pat the fish dry and place on a plate.
   Place the garlic, cayenne, turmeric, salt, and lemon juice in a bowl and mix well to combine the flavors. Smear the fish with this mixture and set aside to marinate for 30 minutes.
   Preheat a broiler to very hot and then lower the heat to medium. Broil the fish for approximately 10 minutes on each side until cooked through.
   Serve hot with a bread or a rich rice dish such as Yogurt with rice (see page 96).

Karwari jheenga/machhi

Goan-style fried fish

This dish is popular on the west coast of India, near Goa. Semolina is used to coat the fish to make a light, crisp coating. It can be served as an appetizer or as part of a main meal

Serves 4
25 shrimp or about 12 ounces monkfish, cut into
  1¹/₂ inch cubes
salt, to taste
1 tablespoon lemon juice
1¹/₂ teaspoons cayenne pepper
1 teaspoon ground turmeric
1¹/₂ teaspoons garlic pulp
2 teaspoons tamarind pulp
1¹/₂ cups semolina
vegetable oil for deep-frying
lemon wedges, to serve

Place the shrimp or monkfish in a bowl with the salt and lemon juice and leave to marinate for about 10 minutes.

Add the cayenne, ground turmeric, garlic pulp, and tamarind pulp. Mix to combine the flavors well and set aside for about 45 minutes.

Place the semolina on a shallow plate. Coat each piece of fish with the semolina and dust off the excess.

Deep-fry in batches in medium-hot oil until golden brown, about 10 minutes. Remove from the oil with a slotted spoon and drain on paper towels. Serve with lemon wedges.

◇ **My tip** I sometimes use fine bread crumbs instead of semolina to coat the fish.

Macchi pattice

Spicy fishcakes

These spicy fishcakes are a favorite of mine, and are a specialty of Bombay, where I grew up.

Serves 4
4 tablespoons (¹/₂ stick) butter
¹/₃ cup chopped onion
¹/₂ teaspoon ground turmeric
2 teaspoons ground coriander
³/₄ teaspoon cayenne pepper
freshly ground black pepper
9 ounces cooked white fish fillet, such as halibut,
  haddock, or sea bass
2 cups cooked basmati rice
3 eggs
salt, to taste
3 tablespoons chopped fresh cilantro
2 cups fresh bread crumbs
all-purpose flour for dusting
vegetable oil for deep-frying

Melt the butter in a skillet. Add the onion, turmeric, coriander, cayenne, and black pepper. Fry gently for about 5 minutes over low heat; set aside to cool.

Place the fish and rice in a food processor or blender and process to a thick paste. Transfer to a large mixing bowl. Add the onion and spice mixture, 1 beaten egg, salt and fresh cilantro and mix well. Divide into 4 equal portions and shape into patties.

Beat the remaining eggs in a shallow dish and place the bread crumbs and flour on separate sheets of waxed paper. Dust the fishcakes with flour, then dip into the egg and coat with bread crumbs, pressing the crumbs on lightly.

Heat the oil in a karhai, wok, or deep skillet and fry the fishcakes in batches for about 5 minutes on each side or until they are golden. Drain well and serve with Cilantro and mint raita (see page 110).

Patra ni macchi

Fish steamed inside a leaf

This is another Parsi dish. Steaming fish in banana leaves reflects an East African influence; they are also used in Thai cooking. Aluminum foil works just as well.

Serves 4

11 ounces fresh coconut, freshly grated

1¹/₂ cups coarsely chopped fresh cilantro

3 tablespoons fresh mint leaves

6 cloves garlic

2 teaspoons cumin seeds

2 tablespoons lemon juice

2 teaspoons sugar

salt, to taste

2 tablespoons vegetable oil

8 to 10 curry leaves

4 banana leaves or squares of aluminum foil, cut into 8-inch squares

1¹/₄ pounds fish fillets, such as halibut, haddock, or sea bass

Place the coconut, cilantro, mint, garlic, and cumin seeds with a little water in a food processor or blender and process to a fine paste. Add the lemon juice, sugar, and salt.

Heat the oil in a small skillet and fry the curry leaves until crisp. Add the leaves and their cooking oil to the coconut paste mixture.

Take a banana leaf or a square of aluminum foil and smother a little of the coconut mixture over it. Place a fillet of fish on top and top with more of the mixture.

Carefully wrap and seal the packages, making sure all the paste is enveloped and nothing can escape; place on a perforated tray.

Place the perforated tray in a steamer and steam for 15 to 20 minutes.

Serve with a chicken dish such as Chicken with fenugreek (see page 58), bread, rice, and vegetables.

Meen kolumbu

Fish curry

This hot-and-sweet dish is popular in the south of India. I've added fennel seeds, which are an eastern influence.

Serves 4

5 tablespoons vegetable oil

4 teaspoons coriander seeds

¹/₂ teaspoon fenugreek seeds

¹/₂ teaspoon fennel seeds

4 red chilies

1³/₄ cups sliced onions

1 ounce tamarind pulp

¹/₂ teaspoon mustard seeds

10 to 12 curry leaves

3 cloves garlic, sliced

¹/₂ teaspoon ground turmeric

³/₄ ounce jaggery or 4 teaspoons brown sugar

salt, to taste

1¹/₄ pounds thick fish steaks (or thick skinless fillets), such as pomfret, halibut, salmon, or swordfish

Heat half the oil in a pan. Add the coriander seeds, fenugreek seeds, fennel seeds, and red chilies. Sauté for 5 minutes until the chilies begin to go dark in color.

Add the sliced onions and fry, stirring constantly, for about 8 minutes. When the onions are soft, remove the mixture and spread onto a tray to cool. When cool, grind to a very fine paste with the tamarind pulp, adding a little water as necessary; set aside.

In a karhai or large, wide skillet, heat the remaining oil. Add the mustard seeds and as soon as they begin to "pop," add the curry leaves, sliced garlic, and turmeric. Add the ground onion paste and stir well. Add water to make a sauce consistency. Add the jaggery and salt.

Bring to a boil. Remove any scum from the surface with a slotted spoon and then add the fish pieces. Cook for approximately 10 minutes until the fish is cooked and flakes easily.

This is often eaten with a chicken dish, such as Black pepper chicken (see page 62).

Chicken, eggs, and meat

Due to religious beliefs, many Indians practice vegetarianism, but meat is eaten throughout the country by some sections of the community. Hinduism prohibits the eating of beef, because they believe the cow is sacred, while pork is forbidden to Muslims. Some sects bend the rules, while others impose additional restrictions, for example, forbidding food that resembles meat, such as tomatoes and beets. Eggs are an excellent source of protein and can be cooked in a number of marvelous ways, but some staunch vegetarians spurn even these.

India, however, does have a rich tradition of meat dishes, with goat, lamb, and chicken being the mainstays. In the north you will find the rich lamb biryanis that were introduced by the Mughals, while Goa is famous for its spicy pork vindaloos. When I was a child I used to travel all over India with my father, and his cook opened up for me a whole new world of exotic meat dishes, many of which I would not normally eat at home. In India, meat is bought in a very different way compared to some other countries—if you are after a chicken you will most likely have to choose one from a basket of live birds. As a rule, in India mutton usually means goat meat, but lamb is a good substitute and not as difficult to find in supermarkets.

Above: **Selecting red chilies in the Koyambedu wholesale market in Chennai.**

Tawa murgh

Chicken with fenugreek

This dish gets its name from the tawa, the flattish, two-handled Indian skillet in which it is cooked, but you can just as easily use any large heavy-bottomed pan. It is very similar to a karhai, and this dish is sometimes also called Karhai murgh.

Serves 4

2 tablespoons vegetable oil

1 teaspoon cumin seeds

2 cups chopped onions

2 teaspoons garlic pulp

1 small green chili, chopped

1½ cups chopped tomatoes

½ teaspoon ground turmeric

¾ teaspoon cayenne pepper

1-inch piece fresh gingerroot, chopped

½ teaspoon black peppercorns, crushed

⅛ teaspoon fenugreek seeds, coarsely ground

12 ounces chicken breast meat, skinned and cut into 1- to 1½-inch cubes

salt, to taste

4 tablespoons (½ stick) butter

7 tablespoons light cream

pinch dried fenugreek leaves (optional)

3 tablespoons chopped fresh cilantro, to garnish

Heat the oil in a tawa, wok, or nonstick skillet. Add the cumin seeds, chopped onions, garlic pulp, and chopped chili and fry until the onions are light brown.

Add the chopped tomatoes, ground turmeric, and cayenne and cook for 10 to 15 minutes until the masala leaves the sides of the tawa and the oil starts to separate.

Stir in the chopped ginger, crushed black peppercorns, and ground fenugreek seeds and then add the chicken pieces. Cook for 15 to 20 minutes over low heat, stirring occasionally; season to taste.

Finish with butter, cream, and dried fenugreek leaves, if using. Sprinkle the

Above: **Chicken with fenugreek served with Okra and potatoes, rice, and chapattis.**

chopped cilantro over and serve with a dal, bread, rice, raita, and a dry vegetable dish, such as Okra and potatoes (see page 88).

Murgh lababdar

Chicken in a creamy tomato and onion sauce

This is a good example of Hyderabadi cuisine and it has also become popular in Delhi and Rajasthan. If you want a slightly milder dish, seed and wash the green chilies before using.

Serves 4 to 6
2 tablespoons vegetable oil
2¹/₂ cups chopped onions
2 tablespoons chopped fresh gingerroot
2 teaspoons garlic pulp
1 small green chili, chopped
1¹/₄ pounds chopped tomatoes
6 tablespoons (³/₄ stick) butter
³/₄ teaspoon cayenne pepper
2¹/₄ pounds chicken breast meat, skinned and cut
   into 1- to 1¹/₂ in cubes
salt, to taste
1¹/₄ cups cream
2 teaspoons garam masala
large pinch of dried fenugreek leaves
3 tablespoons chopped fresh cilantro

Heat the oil in a large heavy-bottomed pan over low heat. Add the chopped onions, ginger, garlic, and green chili and sauté for about 10 minutes until the onions are a light golden brown color.

Add the chopped tomatoes, butter, and cayenne and cook over low heat for about 40 minutes, stirring at regular intervals until the butter separates from the gravy.

Add the chicken pieces and continue to cook for 10 to 15 minutes, or until the chicken is cooked through.

Add the salt and cream and cook for another 10 minutes. Finally, stir in the garam masala and dried fenugreek leaves. Sprinkle with chopped fresh cilantro and serve with Handkerchief-thin bread (see page 99), a vegetable rice dish, and a paneer dish.

Murgh kolhapuri

Aromatic spiced chicken

This comes from Kolhapur in Maharashtra, where the people like their food very spicy and aromatic. The same combination of spices used in this recipe is also used in vegetables dishes.

Serves 4
4 tablespoons vegetable oil
1¹/₂ cups sliced onions
5 teaspoons coriander seeds
1 tablespoon fennel seeds
1 teaspoon black peppercorns
1 teaspoon ground star anise
1 teaspoon ground cardamom
1 teaspoon ground mace
1 cup shredded coconut
1 tablespoon garlic pulp
12 ounces chicken breast meat, skinned and cut into
   1- to 1¹/₂-inch cubes
³/₄ teaspoon cayenne pepper
¹/₂ teaspoon ground turmeric
1 teaspoon ground coriander
salt, to taste

Heat the oil in a karhai, wok, or large skillet and fry the sliced onions for about 10 minutes, or until they turn golden brown.

Add the coriander seeds, fennel seeds, black peppercorns, star anise, cardamom, mace, shredded coconut, and garlic pulp and fry for 3 to 4 minutes over low heat until the flavors have intensified; remove from the heat and set aside.

When the mixture has cooled, place in a food processor or blender and process to a very fine paste. Return to the pan and add more water to make a sauce consistency. Bring to a boil and add the chicken, cayenne, turmeric, ground coriander, and salt. Simmer for 15 to 20 minutes until the chicken is cooked.

Serve with rice or bread or Vegetable biryani (see page 84).

Dhaniya murgh

Coriander chicken

This aromatic dish comes from the north of India. It uses cilantro in all its forms—the crushed seeds, ground coriander, and the fresh leaves of the herb, called cilantro.

Serves 4

2 tablespoons ghee or vegetable oil
1 teaspoon cumin seeds
1$^1/_2$ teaspoons coriander seeds, crushed
1 cup chopped onions
1 tablespoon garlic pulp
1-inch piece fresh gingerroot, cut into
  juliennes
1 green chili, chopped
$^3/_4$ teaspoon ground coriander
14 ounces chicken breast meat, skinned and cut into
  1- to 1$^1/_2$-in cubes
1 cup light cream
1 teaspoon garam masala
3 tablespoons chopped fresh cilantro
salt, to taste

Heat the oil in a large heavy-bottomed pan. Add the cumin seeds and crushed coriander seeds. When they begin to crackle, add the chopped onions and fry for 8 to 10 minutes.

Stir in the garlic pulp, ginger juliennes, and green chili and cook for 2 minutes. Then add the ground coriander, sprinkle with a little water, and cook, stirring, for another couple of minutes.

Add the chicken pieces and sauté for 5 minutes. Add $^1/_2$ cup water, lower the heat, and cook for 5 to 10 minutes. Stir in the cream, garam masala, and most of the chopped fresh cilantro.

Season and cook for 2 to 3 minutes longer. Remove from the heat and sprinkle with the remaining cilantro. Serve with Lentils with cream and butter (see page 106) or Cauliflower with green peas (see page 81).

Murgh malai curry

Coconut chicken curry

The word malai actually means "cream," even though there is no cream in this recipe. It earns the name from its thick coconut sauce, which is wonderfully rich and creamy. I love to eat this with plain boiled rice and pappadums.

Serves 4 to 6

2 tablespoons ghee or vegetable oil
3 cloves
3 green cardamom pods
1 cup chopped onions
3 cloves garlic, crushed
1 tablespoon ground coriander
$^1/_2$ teaspoon mustard powder
1 tablespoon ground cumin
$^3/_4$ teaspoon ground turmeric
$^3/_4$ teaspoon cayenne pepper
1 tablespoon ginger pulp
2$^1/_4$ pounds chicken breast or thigh meat, skinned
  and cut into 1- to 1$^1/_2$-inch cubes
2$^1/_2$ cups coconut milk
salt, to taste
juice of $^1/_2$ lemon

Heat the ghee or oil in a pan and add the whole cloves and cardamom pods. After a minute, add the chopped onion and garlic and fry for 8 to 10 minutes until the onions become soft and translucent.

Add all the ground spices and ginger pulp and sprinkle 2 tablespoons water over. Cook over low heat for 5 minutes. Add the chicken pieces and fry for 2 to 3 minutes longer.

Add the coconut milk and cook over low heat for 25 to 30 minutes until the chicken is cooked. Season and add the lemon juice.

Serve with Green beans with coconut (see page 90), plain rice, bread, and a fresh chutney.

Opposite: **Coconut chicken curry**

Kozhi kurumelagu

Black pepper chicken

This is very popular in southern India. If you
want extra heat, add more black pepper. It is
a wonderfully aromatic dish because of the
cardamom and fennel.

Serves 4

2¹/₂ tablespoons vegetable oil or ghee

2 bay leaves

3 cardamom pods

3 cloves

¹/₂ teaspoon cumin seeds

1¹/₂ cups sliced shallots

1 tablespoon garlic pulp

³/₄ teaspoon ground fennel

2 teaspoons ground coriander

¹/₂ teaspoon ground turmeric

³/₄ teaspoon cayenne pepper

1³/₄ cups chopped tomatoes,

1 pound chicken breast meat, skinned and cut into
    1- to 1¹/₂-in cubes

1¹/₂ teaspoons black peppercorns, crushed

salt, to taste

Heat the oil or ghee in a karhai, wok, or skillet.
When hot, add the whole spices. After a minute,
add the sliced shallots and cook for 5 to 10
minutes until the shallots color. Add the garlic
pulp and cook, stirring, for 1 minute.

Add the fennel, coriander, turmeric, and
cayenne and sprinkle with a little water to
prevent sticking. Cook for 2 minutes longer. Add
the chopped tomatoes and continue to cook,
stirring occasionally, over medium heat for 10 to
15 minutes. Add more water, if required.

Add the chicken pieces and continue to cook
for 15 to 20 minutes over low heat. Add the
crushed black pepper and season.

Right: **Chicken with spinach with Rice flavored with cumin
seeds (see page 97)**

Saagwala murgh
Chicken with spinach

"Saag" usually means spinach, but I sometimes use other leafy vegetables, such as watercress or mustard leaves. This goes beautifully with Rice flavored with cumin seeds (see page 97).

Serves 4

10 ounces spinach leaves
2¹⁄₂ tablespoons ghee or vegetable oil
2 bay leaves
3 cloves
3 cardamom pods
1 teaspoon cumin seeds
1 cup chopped onions
5 cloves garlic, finely chopped
1 green chili, chopped
¹⁄₂ teaspoon ground turmeric
2 tomatoes, skinned and diced
14 ounces chicken breast meat, skinned and cut into
  1- to 1¹⁄₂-inch cubes
¹⁄₄ cup light cream
salt, to taste
1 teaspoon garam masala
2 tablespoons chopped fresh cilantro

Blanch the spinach leaves in boiling water for 2 minutes, then drain and puree in a food processor.

Heat the ghee or oil in a karhai, wok, or large skillet. Add the whole spices and when they begin to crackle, add the chopped onions and fry for 8 to 10 minutes until the onions begin to change color.

Add the chopped garlic and green chili and continue to fry. Add the turmeric and diced tomatoes and fry for 2 minutes.

Add the chicken pieces and cook for 3 minutes over medium heat. Add the pureed spinach and continue to cook over low heat for 15 to 20 minutes until the chicken is cooked.

Stir in the cream and season. Sprinkle the garam masala and chopped cilantro over and cook for 2 minutes longer before serving.

Tariwali murgh

Chicken simmered in a tomato sauce

This is a very popular dish in northern India and is wonderfully aromatic. It takes its Indian name from the way it is cooked.

Serves 4

vegetable oil for deep-frying
2¼ cups sliced onions
2 cups chopped tomatoes, or 1 can (7 ounces), crushed
2½ tablespoons vegetable oil or ghee
1 teaspoon cumin seeds
4 cardamom pods
4 cloves
3 bay leaves
1 tablespoon garlic pulp
½ teaspoon ground turmeric
¾ teaspoon cayenne pepper
1 teaspoon ground paprika
1 pound chicken breast meat, skinned and cut into 1- to 1½-inch cubes
1 teaspoon ground fennel
1 teaspoon sugar
salt, to taste
1 tablespoon plain yogurt
light cream (optional)
chopped fresh cilantro, to garnish

Heat the oil in a large heavy-bottomed pan to 375°F. Deep-fry the sliced onions until they turn golden, stirring frequently. Remove with a slotted spoon and drain on paper towels. Put the fried onions and chopped tomatoes in a food processor or blender and process to a smooth paste; set aside.

In another pan, heat the oil or ghee and add the cumin seeds, cardamom pods, cloves, and bay leaves. When they begin to crackle, add the garlic pulp, turmeric, cayenne, and paprika. Sprinkle with a little water and cook, stirring, for 3 to 5 minutes over low heat. If the spices start to stick to the bottom of the pan, sprinkle with a little water and keep stirring.

Stir in the tomato and onion paste and cook over low heat for 5 to 10 minutes. Add the chicken pieces and cook over low heat for 15 to 20 minutes, stirring occasionally. Add a little water if the sauce becomes too thick. Stir in the ground fennel.

When the chicken is cooked, add the sugar, salt, and yogurt and remove from the heat. Garnish with a swirl of cream, if using, and sprinkle with the chopped cilantro.

Murgh mirch masala

Chicken with peppers

This is a colorful dish from the north of India. A southern version of this recipe would use more crushed black pepper and no cream—you can adapt it to your own taste.

Serves 4 to 6

2 tablespoons vegetable oil or ghee
1 teaspoon cumin seeds
2 cloves
2 cardamom pods
generous 1 cup chopped onions
2 teaspoons garlic pulp
¾ teaspoon cayenne pepper
2 teaspoons ground coriander
½ teaspoon ground turmeric
1½ cups chopped tomatoes
14 ounces chicken breast meat, skinned and cut into 1- to 1½-in cubes
1 red bell pepper, sliced
1 yellow bell pepper, sliced
1 green bell pepper, sliced
1 green chili, chopped
1 teaspoon black peppercorns, crushed
¼ cup light cream
½ teaspoon sugar
2 tablespoons chopped fresh cilantro
salt, to taste

Heat the oil or ghee in a karhai, wok, or skillet. When hot, add the cumin seeds, cloves, and cardamom pods. When they begin to crackle, add the chopped onions and cook over medium heat for 10 to12 minutes.

Add the garlic pulp and cook, stirring, for 2 minutes. Stir in the ground spices and chopped tomatoes and cook for 10 to 15 minutes until the oil begins to separate. If the mixture starts to stick to the pan, sprinkle a little water over. Add the chicken and sliced peppers and cook for

Above: **Chicken with peppers**

10 to 15 minutes longer. Stir in the remaining ingredients, reserving some cilantro to garnish. Season and cook for 5 to 10 minutes longer. Serve sprinkled with the remaining cilantro.

Anda bhurjee

Spicy scrambled eggs

This is a great brunch dish which can also be part of a main meal. As a child I used to love eating it in bread and butter, like a sandwich. It's really a sort of spicy Spanish omelet, which you can adapt to make hotter. It originated in the north, but is now eaten all over India.

Serves 4

6 eggs
2 tablespoons milk
salt, to taste
1/2 teaspoon ground black pepper
3 tablespoons vegetable oil
scant 1 cup chopped onions
1/4 teaspoon ground turmeric
1 green chili, chopped
1/2 teaspoon ground cumin
1 tomato, skinned, seeded and
** finely diced**
1 tablespoon chopped fresh cilantro

Break the eggs into a bowl, add the milk, salt and pepper, and whisk well.

Put the oil in a nonstick skillet and place over medium heat. When hot, add the chopped onions, turmeric, green chili, and cumin. Cook, stirring, for 3 to 5 minutes Add half the diced tomatoes and cook for 1 minute.

Pour in the egg mixture and cook, stirring vigorously with a wooden spoon to avoid the egg sticking to the pan. Sprinkle with half the chopped cilantro and continue to cook until the eggs are done to your taste. Garnish with the remaining diced tomato and cilantro and serve.

Baida curry

Egg curry

As most Indians are nonmeat eaters, eggs are a great way of providing necessary protein. I love this recipe—it is quick to make and perfect with chapattis or parathas for brunch, or with rice for a light supper. You can also serve an onion, cilantro, chili, lemon, and salt salad on the side.

Serves 4

6 eggs
2 tablespoons vegetable oil or ghee
1 teaspoon cumin seeds
1/2 teaspoon mustard seeds
2 bay leaves
8 to 10 curry leaves (optional)
3 cloves
3 cardamom pods
generous 1 cup sliced onions
1 tablespoon garlic pulp
1 tablespoon ginger pulp
1 tablespoon ground coriander
3/4 teaspoon cayenne pepper
1/2 teaspoon ground turmeric
13/4 cups chopped tomatoes
1/2 teaspoon garam masala
salt, to taste
2 tablespoons chopped fresh cilantro

Hard-boil the eggs, shell, cut into quarters, and arrange in the base of a serving dish; set aside.

Heat the oil or ghee in a karhai or wok. Add the cumin seeds, mustard seeds, bay leaves, curry leaves, if using, cloves, and cardamom pods. When they begin to crackle, add the sliced onions and fry for 10 to 12 minutes.

Stir in the garlic, ginger, coriander, cayenne, and turmeric. Sprinkle with a little water and cook, stirring, for 2 minutes. Add the chopped tomatoes and garam masala and cook over low heat for 10 to 15 minutes. If the contents of the pan start to stick, add a little more water; season. Pour the sauce over the eggs in the serving dish and sprinkle with the fresh cilantro.

Opposite: **Egg curry**

Kheema kofta curry

Lamb meatballs in a spicy sauce

This is very much a specialty of the northwest region and was originally introduced by the Mughal emperors. There are many variations but this is my preferred recipe.

Serves 4
For the koftas:
9 ounces ground lamb
1 chopped onion
1 tablespoon garlic pulp
1 tablespoon ginger pulp
3/4 teaspoon cayenne pepper
1 teaspoon ground coriander
2 tablespoons chopped fresh cilantro
1 egg, beaten
salt, to taste

For the sauce:
2 tablespoons tomato paste
6 tablespoons plain yogurt
1 tablespoon vegetable oil
1 teaspoon cumin seeds
1 bay leaf
1 tablespoon garlic pulp
2 teaspoons ginger pulp
1/2 teaspoon ground turmeric
3/4 teaspoon cayenne pepper
salt, to taste
3/4 teaspoon garam masala

To make the koftas, place the ground lamb in a food processor or blender and process for about 1 minute; remove and set aside in a large bowl.

Place the onions, garlic, ginger, cayenne, ground coriander, and half of the chopped fresh cilantro in the food processor and blend together for about 1 minute. Combine with the ground lamb. Add the egg and season; set aside for 1 hour.

To make the sauce, beat together the tomato paste and yogurt; set aside. Heat the oil in a pan and, when hot, add the cumin seeds and bay

leaf. When the seeds begin to crackle, add the garlic and ginger. Cook, for 1 minute. Add the turmeric and cayenne and then the yogurt mixture. Add salt and cook for 2 minutes longer.

Take small balls of ground-meat mixture and shape into small koftas (round ball shapes) using well-greased hands. Return the sauce to high heat and add the koftas. Cover and cook for about 15 minutes, stirring occasionally.

Serve hot, sprinkled with the garam masala and remaining chopped cilantro.

Kheema bhurjee

Ground lamb with peas and mint

This is a wonderfully simple and comforting dish and is great served with rice or chapattis. You can also use ground beef, but I prefer lamb. If you can buy a good cut and grind it yourself, you will really notice the difference in taste.

Serves 4
2 tablespoons vegetable oil
2/3 cup chopped onions
1/2 teaspoon cumin seeds
2 bay leaves
1 tablespoon garlic pulp
1 tablespoon ginger pulp
3/4 teaspoon cayenne pepper
1/2 teaspoon ground turmeric
2 teaspoons ground coriander
1/2 cup shelled peas, thawed if frozen
1 1/2 cups chopped tomatoes
12 ounces ground lamb
1 tablespoon chopped fresh mint
2 tablespoons chopped fresh cilantro
1 green chili, chopped
salt, to taste

Heat the oil in a karhai, wok, or large heavy-bottomed skillet. Add the onions and cook over medium heat for 10 to 15 minutes, or until golden brown, then add the cumin seeds and bay leaves.

In a bowl, combine the garlic pulp, ginger pulp,

cayenne, ground turmeric, ground coriander, peas, and chopped fresh tomatoes. Add this mixture to the cooked onions in the pan and cook, stirring constantly, for about 5 minutes.

Add the ground lamb to the mixture and stir-fry for 10 to 15 minutes. Stir in the chopped

Above: **Ground lamb with peas and mint**

mint, most of the chopped cilantro and the green chili and mix well. Season.

Stir-fry for another 2 to 3 minutes and serve garnished with the remaining chopped cilantro.

Irachi varthathu

Dry-fried lamb with spices

This dish comes from Kerala on the southernmost tip of India. The spices will make it very hot, but beautifully aromatic. I serve this with plain boiled rice and a cooling yogurt relish.

Serves 4 to 6

4 tablespoons vegetable oil

2 dried red chilies

3 cloves

3 green cardamom pods

2 cinnamon sticks

1 teaspoon cumin seeds

1 teaspoon fennel seeds

8 to 10 black peppercorns

2 bay leaves

25 curry leaves

2 cups sliced onions

6 to 8 cloves garlic, crushed

1-inch piece fresh gingerroot, sliced

2¼ pounds boned shoulder of lamb, cut into
    1- to 1½-inch cubes

1 tablespoon ground coriander

½ teaspoon ground turmeric

¾ teaspoon cayenne pepper

salt, to taste

2 tablespoons shredded coconut

fried curry leaves and shredded coconut, to garnish

Heat the oil in a karhai, wok, or large heavy-bottomed skillet. When hot, add all the whole spices and curry leaves. When they begin to crackle, add the sliced onions and cook until golden brown in color. Add the garlic and ginger and cook, stirring, for another 2 minutes.

Add the diced lamb and cook over high heat until the lamb colors, 5 to 10 minutes. Add the ground spices and cook, stirring frequently, for about 10 minutes. Cover and cook over low heat for 10 to 15 minutes longer.

Season and stir in the shredded coconut. Serve garnished with more coconut and fried curry leaves.

Bhuna gosht

Stir-fried lamb with onions

Mutton really is the best meat for this dish, so if you can get hold of some from your butcher, do use it. However, lamb is a perfectly good substitute. This dish gets its name from the method of cooking—bhuna means "stir-fried."

Serves 4 to 6

3 tablespoons vegetable oil

1 teaspoon cumin seeds

6 cardamom pods

6 cloves

3 bay leaves

2¾ cups sliced onions

1 tablespoon garlic pulp

1-inch piece fresh gingerroot, cut into juliennes

1½ teaspoons cayenne pepper

4 teaspoons ground coriander

¾ teaspoon ground turmeric

2¼ pounds mutton or lamb, cut into
    1- to 1½-inch cubes

salt, to taste

6 tablespoons plain yogurt

2 tablespoons chopped fresh cilantro

Heat the oil in a large heavy-bottomed pan. Add the cumin seeds, cardamom pods, cloves, and bay leaves. When the cumin seeds begin to crackle, add the sliced onions and cook over medium heat for 15 to 20 minutes until the onions are nicely browned.

Stir in the garlic, ginger, cayenne, ground coriander, and turmeric. Add the mutton or lamb cubes, reduce the heat, and cook, stirring constantly, for approximately 30 minutes. Add the salt and yogurt and cook for 5 minutes longer. Stir in half the chopped cilantro.

Serve hot, sprinkled with the remaining chopped fresh cilantro.

Kalimiri gosht

Lamb in a black pepper sauce

This is really a very spicy dish and a favorite with those who like heat and spice. Black pepper is a great flavor enhancer, but in increased quantities will give a real kick to a dish.

Serves 4 to 6

5 teaspoons coriander seeds
5 teaspoons cumin seeds
2 teaspoons black cumin seeds
1 tablespoon black peppercorns
a few saffron strands
1 cup plain yogurt
salt, to taste
2¼ pounds boned shoulder of lamb, cut into
    1- to 1½-inch cubes
²⁄₃ cup ghee
5 green cardamom pods
1 black cardamom pod
5 cloves
1-inch piece of cinnamon stick
1 bay leaf
1³⁄₄ cups sliced onions
1-inch piece fresh gingerroot, chopped
2 green chilies, chopped
1 cup light cream
1 teaspoon ground fennel

Using a mortar and pestle, crush together the coriander seeds, cumin seeds, black cumin seeds, and black peppercorns. Dissolve the saffron in 2 tablespoons of lukewarm water; set aside.

Mix the crushed spices with the yogurt and salt and use it to cover the lamb pieces. Leave to marinate for at least 30 minutes.

Heat the ghee in a karhai, wok, or large heavy-bottomed skillet. Add the cardamom pods, cloves, cinnamon, and bay leaf and cook over medium heat until the spices begin to crackle. Add the onions and cook until they turn golden brown, 15 to 20 minutes.

Add the ginger and green chilies to the pan and cook, stirring, for 1 minute. Add the marinated lamb pieces and stir to combine. Add 3 cups water and bring to a boil. Cover and simmer for 25 to 30 minutes.

Add the saffron liquid and cream and bring back to a boil. Adjust the seasoning, sprinkle with the ground fennel, and serve hot.

Gosht biryani

Layered lamb biryani

Biryani is the lasting legacy of the Mughals who once ruled India. These fragrant rice and meat dishes can be eaten as a complete meal. This version would be served for a special occasion, although it is surprisingly easy to make.

Serves 4 to 6

1¼ cups basmati rice
5 tablespoons vegetable oil or ghee
4 cloves
4 cardamom pods
a few saffron strands
¼ cup plain yogurt
salt, to taste
1 tablespoon garlic pulp
1½ teaspoons ginger pulp
½ teaspoon ground turmeric
1 tablespoon ground coriander
1 teaspoon ground fennel
1½ pounds boneless lamb meat, such as leg, cut into
    1-inch cubes
1 cup sliced onions
1 can (7 ounces) crushed tomatoes
2 tablespoons chopped fresh cilantro
2 tablespoons chopped fresh mint
sliced fried onions and chopped fresh cilantro,
    to garnish

Wash the rice in several changes of water and set aside. Take two large pans and to each add 1 tablespoon of oil, 2 cloves, and 2 cardamom pods, but put the saffron strands in only one pan. Divide the washed rice equally between the 2 pans. Cover the rice in each pan with boiling water and cook over medium-high heat for 12 to 15 minutes, or until the rice is cooked; drain separately and set aside.

Above: **Layered lamb biryani**

Mix together the yogurt, salt, garlic pulp, ginger pulp, and ground spices in a large bowl. Add the cubes of lamb and leave to marinate for at least 1 hour.

In another pan, heat the remaining oil or ghee and fry the sliced onions for 8 to 10 minutes, or until golden. Add the crushed tomatoes and the marinated lamb and cook, covered, for 30 minutes, stirring occasionally. Add salt and the chopped cilantro and mint. Cook over high heat to reduce down to a thick sauce.

Use a well-greased ovenproof dish or bowl and layer the bottom first with boiled rice and then with saffron rice. Spread a layer of lamb mixture over this followed by another layer of the two different rice mixes. Repeat until all the lamb is used, making sure that the top layer is rice. Place the dish in a heated oven for 5 minutes so the flavors blend together.

To serve, you will need to invert the dish carefully over a large plate and then gently remove. Garnish with the browned onions and chopped fresh cilantro.

Achaari gosht

Lamb in a pickled spice sauce

This is a popular dish in western India, but is eaten in the north as well. The long list of spices means that this is a wonderfully aromatic dish.

Serves 4 to 6

2 onions
2-inch piece fresh gingerroot, chopped
8 cloves garlic, chopped
1 bay leaf
2 black cardamom pods
2 tablespoons coriander seeds
¼ teaspoon fenugreek seeds
2 cinnamon sticks
5 cloves
1 teaspoon cumin seeds
pinch of onion seeds
½ teaspoon mustard seeds
2 black peppercorns
7 green chilies
6 tablespoons ghee or vegetable oil
2¼ pounds boned shoulder of lamb, cut into
  1- to 1½-inch cubes
¼ teaspoon ground turmeric
¾ teaspoon cayenne pepper
6 tablespoons plain yogurt
salt, to taste
1 tablespoon chopped fresh cilantro

Chop 1 of the onions and put in a food processor or blender with the ginger, garlic, and a little water; process to a smooth paste.

Using a mortar and pestle, crush together the whole spices. Slit the green chilies in half and set aside.

Heat the ghee or oil in a heavy-bottomed pan over medium heat. Add the crushed spices and stir-fry for 1 minute. Slice the other onion and add to the pan. Cook, stirring, for 10 to 15 minutes, or until it turns golden brown.

Add the lamb pieces and stir-fry for 4 to 8 minutes. Stir in the ginger, garlic, and onion paste and cook for 10 minutes longer. Add the ground

turmeric, cayenne, and yogurt, cover, and gently simmer for about 20 minutes. Add the green chilies and continue to cook over low heat for 15 to 20 minutes or until the lamb is tender; season to taste.

Serve hot garnished with chopped cilantro.

Salli jardaloo boti

Lamb with apricots and fried potato straws

A traditional Parsi dish that would be prepared for weddings and other religious ceremonies. As always, you can reduce the heat, if you like, by seeding the chilies.

Serves 4 to 6

4 dried red chilies, diced
2-inch piece of cinnamon stick
2½ teaspoons cumin seeds
6 cardamom pods
8 cloves
2 teaspoons ginger pulp
2 teaspoons garlic pulp
2¼ pounds boned shoulder of lamb, cut into
  1- to 1½-inch cubes
10 to 15 dried apricots, roughly chopped
5 tablespoons vegetable oil
2 cups sliced onions
1 cup chopped tomatoes
salt, to taste
2 tablespoons white-wine vinegar
2 tablespoons sugar

For the potato straws (salli):
2 teaspoons salt
1 large potato, peeled
vegetable oil for deep-frying

Using a coffee or spice grinder, blend together the red chilies, cinnamon sticks, cumin seeds, cardamom pods, and cloves to a very fine powder. Mix together half the ginger, half the garlic, and half the ground spices. Rub the lamb pieces with this mixture and leave to marinate for at least 1 hour.

Place the apricots in a pan with about 2¼ cups water and bring to a boil. Leave to soak in their cooking water for about 30 minutes, or until they become soft and mushy.

Heat the oil in a karhai, wok, or large heavy-bottomed skillet and fry the sliced onions over medium heat for 15 to 20 minutes until they turn a rich brown color. Add the remaining ginger, garlic, and ground spices and cook, stirring, for 2 minutes.

Add the lamb and stir-fry for about 5 minutes. Stir in the chopped tomatoes and salt. Add the vinegar, sugar, apricot mixture, and a little water, stir and simmer over low heat for 25 minutes until the lamb is tender.

To make the potato straws, add the salt to about 2 cups water. Cut the peeled potato into very fine strips and put into the water for 5 minutes. Heat the oil in a large pan or wok. Squeeze the potato strips to remove as much water as possible and fry in the oil until golden brown. Remove and drain on paper towels.

To serve, heat the lamb gently and garnish with the potato straws.

Below: **Lamb with apricots and fried potato straws**

Bade aur mirch ki curry

Beef-chili curry

Although beef is forbidden to Hindus, the Anglo-Indians in Goa do eat it. Being lovers of hot dishes, they use chilies in every form—this dish has fresh green chilies, cayenne, and a red chili garnish!

Serves 4

generous 1 cup chopped onions
5 cloves garlic, chopped
1/2-inch piece fresh gingerroot, chopped
3/4 teaspoon cayenne pepper
1/2 teaspoon ground turmeric
1 teaspoon ground coriander
1 teaspoon ground cumin
12 ounces stewing beef, cut into
    1- to 11/2-inch cubes
salt, to taste
3 tablespoons vegetable oil
3 green chilies, slit lengthwise
red chilies, to garnish

Place half the onions, the garlic cloves, and chopped ginger in a food processor or blender and grind to a fine paste. Add the ground spices to this paste and combine well. Smear the cubed beef with roughly half the paste and sprinkle with salt. Leave to marinate for 10 to 15 minutes. Set aside the remaining paste.

Heat half the oil in a large heavy-bottomed pan. Add the remaining chopped onions and the beef. Cook, stirring, for about 5 minutes. Remove from the pan with a slotted spoon and set aside. Add the remaining oil to the pan and stir-fry the green chilies with the remaining paste for 5 to 6 minutes over medium heat.

Return the beef and onions to the pan with about 1/2 cup water. Cook over high heat for 3 to 4 minutes. Add salt and simmer for 10 minutes longer, stirring occasionally and adding more water, if necessary.

When the beef is cooked, serve with plain boiled rice and garnish with fresh red chilies.

Vindaloo

Beef/pork cooked in vinegar and garlic

This is an authentically east Indian dish from Goa, and was probably invented by the Portuguese who settled there. Famous for being searingly hot, it is delicious with plain boiled rice.

Serves 4

1 pound boneless beef or pork, cut into
    1- to 11/2-inch cubes
2 tablespoons vinegar
salt, to taste
2 tablespoons vegetable oil
4 cloves garlic, crushed
13/4 cups sliced onions
1 cup chopped tomatoes
4 green chilies, slit lengthwise
1/2 teaspoon sugar

For the spice paste:
6 dried red chilies
2 teaspoons bright red paprika
1/2 teaspoon ground turmeric
1 teaspoon cumin seeds
2-inch piece of cinnamon stick
10 cloves
10 to 12 black peppercorns
5 cardamom pods
10 cloves garlic
11/2-inch piece fresh gingerroot, chopped

Place the cubed meat in a large bowl, cover with half the vinegar and some salt, and place in the refrigerator for 2 hours.

Place all the spice paste ingredients and the remaining vinegar in a food processor or blender and grind to a fine paste. Rub half of the paste over the meat and marinate in the refrigerator for 8 to 10 hours longer.

Heat the oil in a large heavy-bottomed pan and add the crushed garlic. When it begins to change color, add the sliced onions and cook until they are golden brown. Add the chopped tomatoes, the remaining spice paste, green chili,

and sugar. Cook over medium heat for
10 to 15 minutes.

Add the marinated meat and about 1 cup
water and cook over medium heat for 20 to 25
minutes. Add salt to taste. After 5 to 10 minutes
check if the meat is tender and cooked; the sauce
should have the consistency of thick cream.

Above: **Beef-chili curry**

Vegetable dishes

Indian fruit and vegetable markets are truly inspiring and a trip to the market is an important part of the food culture—when I was a child I marveled at the colorful stalls and learned how to select the best produce and bargain with the sellers. The eating habits of Indians vary enormously depending on religion and region, but one thing links us all—our love for vegetables. If you are Indian, it is almost taken for granted that you are vegetarian, but even when you do eat meat you would almost certainly have at least two or three vegetable dishes with it. Vegetables are not really eaten as an accompaniment in the same way as they are in the West. A typical meal for a true vegetarian would be several vegetable dishes that use a range of different ingredients and, thereby, provide a balanced meal. Spinach leaves and other greens are cooked with paneer. Potatoes are a popular staple throughout India, while cauliflower, okra, cabbage, corn, eggplants, and beans are prepared in a thousand different ways. Lesser-known vegetables such as karela (bitter melon) and doodhi (Indian pumpkin) are also popular, but it would take forever to name every vegetable. Here are some of my favorite vegetable dishes.

Above: **An early morning at the Koyambedu wholesale market in Chennai.** *Above right:* **Some of the more interesting, as well as the familiar, vegetables on offer.** *Opposite:* **A typical market in Kerala.**

Adraki gobi

Cauliflower with ginger

This dish is eaten all over India. It would most likely be served with other dishes as part of a main meal. Cauliflower is a favorite in my family and because my husband is vegetarian, I cook it for him often.

Serves 4

2-inch piece fresh gingerroot
1 tablespoon vegetable oil
1/2 teaspoon cumin seeds
3/4 cup chopped onions
1/2 teaspoon garlic pulp
1 green chili, finely chopped
1/4 teaspoon ground turmeric
1/4 teaspoon ground coriander
1/2 teaspoon ground ginger
1 pound 5 ounces cauliflower, cut into flowerets
salt, to taste
1 teaspoon ground cumin
3 tablespoons chopped fresh cilantro
1 teaspoon lemon juice

Make a pulp with half of the ginger and cut the remaining half into julienne strips; set aside separately.

Heat the oil in a large pan and add the cumin seeds. When they begin to crackle, add the onions, followed by the garlic pulp and cook over medium heat, stirring, for 10 to 12 minutes.

Add the ginger pulp and green chili. Cook for 1 minute, then add the ground turmeric, ground coriander, and ground ginger, followed by a sprinkle of water. Add the cauliflower and salt and cook over low heat for 10 to 15 minutes or until the cauliflower is cooked. It should still retain some bite.

Adjust the seasoning and sprinkle with the ground cumin, some of the chopped cilantro (leaving some for a garnish), and the lemon juice.

Serve hot, garnished with more chopped cilantro and the ginger julienne strips.

Cachumbar

Cucumber, tomato, and onion salad

This is a very popular Indian salad from Gujarat, which is served as an accompaniment in most Indian houses. There are many different combinations, but the recipe below is probably the most popular and the one I make at home.

Serves 4

3 green chilies
1 3/4 cups red onions, peeled and finely chopped
1 cup firm red tomatoes, cut into small wedges
3/4 cup peeled and diced cucumber
2 tablespoons chopped fresh cilantro
3 tablespoons lemon juice
1 teaspoon black mustard seeds, coarsely crushed
1 teaspoon sugar
salt, to taste

Chop the green chilies. Seed them first if you want the salad to be less hot.

Combine all the ingredients in a bowl and toss well. Cover and keep at room temperature for at least 15 to 20 minutes before serving so the flavors develop.

◇ **My tip** If you have any cachumbar left over, it is delicious added to plain yogurt to make a raita. Add some more chopped cilantro and a couple of pinches of red chili flakes and refrigerate for a couple of hours.

Gobi mutter

Cauliflower with green peas

This beautifully colorful dish comes from northern India and is a typical Gujarati recipe. It is also eaten in East India, where cooks add more garam masala.

Serves 4
3 tablespoons vegetable oil
1 teaspoon cumin seeds
2 teaspoons garlic pulp
1 teaspoon chopped fresh gingerroot
1 small green chili, chopped
1/2 teaspoon ground turmeric
1 1/4 pounds cauliflower, cut into flowerets
1 cup shelled peas, thawed if frozen
salt, to taste
2 tablespoons chopped fresh cilantro
1/2 teaspoon ground cumin
1/2 teaspoon garam masala
juice of 1/2 lemon

Heat the oil in a karhai, wok, or large pan. When hot, add the cumin seeds, followed by the garlic, ginger, and green chili.

Add the ground turmeric, cauliflower, peas, and salt. Sprinkle with a little water, stir, cover the pan, and cook for 10 to 15 minutes.

When the cauliflower is cooked, stir in the chopped fresh cilantro, ground cumin, garam masala, and lemon juice. Mix well and serve immediately.

◇ **My tip** Fresh shelled peas are best for this recipe, but you can use frozen peas or even sliced snow peas or thin green beans.

Left: **Cauliflower with green peas**

Batata nu saak

Spicy potatoes in a tomato sauce

This dish comes from Gujarat, where the local people love sweet, spicy, and sour flavorings. Originally, it would not have had the curry leaves and the shredded coconut. Serve for brunch with pooris or for a main meal with Rice flavored with cumin seeds (see page 97), plain yogurt, and mango pickle.

Serves 4

4 tablespoons vegetable oil
³/₄ teaspoon mustard seeds
1 teaspoon cumin seeds
¹/₂ teaspoon dried red chilies
¹/₄ teaspoon ground asafoetida
10 to 12 curry leaves
3 cups peeled and diced potatoes
³/₄ teaspoon cayenne pepper
¹/₂ teaspoon ground turmeric
2 teaspoons ginger pulp
1 green chili, chopped
1 cup chopped tomatoes
¹/₂ teaspoon ground coriander
1 tablespoon shredded coconut
1 ounce jaggery, or 2 tablespoons brown sugar
salt, to taste
³/₄ ounce tamarind paste
2 tablespoons chopped fresh cilantro

Heat the oil in a pan. Add the mustard seeds, cumin seeds, dried red chilies, and asafoetida. After 1 minute, add the curry leaves and stir.

Add the potatoes, cayenne, ground turmeric, ginger, and green chili. Stir-fry over high heat for about 30 seconds. Add 1 cup water, cover, and simmer for 5 minutes.

Stir in the chopped tomatoes, ground coriander, coconut, jaggery, and salt and cook for 10 minutes. Add the tamarind paste and half of the chopped cilantro and cook for 2 minutes longer. Sprinkle with the remaining chopped cilantro and serve.

Kaikari ishtu

Vegetables in coconut milk

The coconut milk in this dish tells you that it originated in southern India, where coconut milk is used extensively in cooking. The vegetables used can vary—here I've used potatoes, cauliflower, carrots, and peas. I would eat this dish with plain boiled rice, chapattis, or uttapam. It also makes a great accompaniment to a fish curry.

Serves 4

4 tablespoons vegetable oil
³/₄ teaspoon mustard seeds
10 to 12 curry leaves
1-inch piece fresh gingerroot, cut into juliennes
1¹/₂ cups sliced onions
2 green chilies, slit lengthwise
2 potatoes, peeled and cut into ¹/₂-inch dice
2 carrots, peeled and cut into ¹/₂-inch dice
1 cup small cauliflower flowerets
2¹/₄ cups coconut milk
1 cup shelled peas, thawed if frozen
1 teaspoon sugar
salt, to taste
2 tablespoons rice flour
fried curry leaves, to garnish

Heat the oil in a large pan. When hot, add the mustard seeds. When they begin to crackle, add the curry leaves, ginger juliennes, and sliced onions. Cook, stirring, for 5 minutes, then add the green chilies. Add the potatoes, carrots, and cauliflower and stir together.

Pour the coconut milk into the pan and add the peas. Cook for 10 to 15 minutes, or until the vegetables are tender. Add the sugar and salt.

Mix the rice flour with 7 tablespoons water and use to thicken the sauce. Add a little at a time, stirring all the time until the sauce is the consistency of thin cream. Garnish with fried curry leaves and serve immediately.

Dindigul biryani

Vegetable biryani

This dish is from Dindigul, in southern India. Dindigul prides itself on its very own biryani recipe, which is sold from stalls on the streets.

Serves 4 to 6

1¼ cups basmati rice

5 tablespoons vegetable oil

3 cloves

3 cardamom pods

1 cup sliced onions

1 tablespoon garlic pulp

2 teaspoons ginger pulp

¾ teaspoon cayenne pepper

2 teaspoons ground coriander

1 teaspoon ground fennel

1⅓ cups chopped tomatoes

½ cup carrots cut into 1-inch pieces

½ cup green beans cut into 1-inch pieces

4 ounces cauliflower flowerets

7 tablespoons coconut milk

salt, to taste

3 tablespoons chopped fresh cilantro

fried curry leaves and plain boiled rice, to garnish

Wash the rice in several changes of water; leave to soak in a large pan of water.

Heat the oil in a large pan and add the cloves and cardamom pods. After 1 minute, add the sliced onions and fry for 10 to 15 minutes until the onions are soft and change color.

Stir in the garlic, ginger, and the ground spices. Sprinkle with water and cook, stirring, for 5 to 10 minutes. Add the chopped tomatoes and continue to cook over medium heat for 5 to 8 minutes until the oil begins to separate.

Drain the rice and add to the pan with the carrots, green beans, and cauliflower flowerets. Cook, stirring, for 2 minutes. Add the coconut milk and sufficient water to cover the rice by ½-inch. Season and stir in the chopped cilantro. Cover, reduce the heat, and simmer for 15 minutes until the water has been absorbed.

Transfer to a serving dish and garnish with fried curry leaves and a few grains of plain boiled rice.

Ras gobi dhana shaak

Cauliflower with fresh cilantro and tomato

This dish comes from Bombay, in western India, where I grew up. My grandmother's cook taught me this recipe—it is one of the first things I learned to cook.

Serves 4

1 tablespoon vegetable oil
1 teaspoon black mustard seeds
3 chopped tomatoes into large chunks
1 tablespoon ground coriander
1/2 tablespoon ground cumin
1/2 teaspoon ground turmeric
2 tablespoons Cilantro, chili, garlic, and ginger paste (see page 20)
2 pounds cauliflower, cut into flowerets
3 tablespoons chopped fresh cilantro
salt, to taste

Heat the vegetable oil in a large pan, karhai, or wok. When the oil just begins to smoke, add the mustard seeds. Keep a splatter lid handy so the seeds do not start jumping out of the pan.

Immediately add the tomatoes, ground coriander, ground cumin, and ground turmeric and the Cilantro, chili, garlic, and ginger paste. Cover and cook slowly for 2 minutes, or until the tomatoes have softened.

Add the cauliflower, chopped cilantro, and 1 cup water. Stir well, cover, and cook for 5 minutes. Remove the lid and cook over medium heat for 2 minutes longer. Season and serve immediately.

◇ **My tip** I always use the stems of the cilantro herb, as well as the leaves, because it adds a lot of flavor to the dish. I don't like waste!

Left: **Vegetable biryani**

Makai jalfrezi

Baby corn jalfrezi

Baby corn is a relatively new vegetable to India, but it is now grown extensively around Calcutta, where this dish comes from. As you travel farther north up the river Ganges the flavors change.

Serves 4

14 ounces baby corn cobs, slit lengthwise
11 ounces tomatoes
2¹/₂ tablespoons vegetable oil
¹/₄ teaspoon cumin seeds
1³/₄ cups finely sliced onions
¹/₂ teaspoon garlic pulp
1-inch piece fresh gingerroot, chopped
1 green chili, finely chopped
³/₄ teaspoon cayenne pepper
¹/₂ teaspoon ground turmeric
3 tablespoons tomato paste
salt, to taste
1 tablespoon white-wine vinegar
1 cup green bell pepper, cut into strips
1 teaspoon East Indian garam masala (see page 23)
3 tablespoons chopped fresh cilantro

Cook the baby corn cobs in boiling water for 2 minutes: Do not overcook them, because you want them to be crunchy. Place half the tomatoes in a food processor or blender and process until you have a smooth puree; strain and set aside. Cut the remaining tomatoes into strips.

Heat 2 tablespoons of the oil in a large pan and add the cumin seeds. When they begin to crackle, add the onions and garlic. Add the ginger and green chili and cook for 3 to 4 minutes. Stir in the cayenne, ground turmeric, tomato paste, and baby corn cobs and cook for 5 to 8 minutes. Add the salt and vinegar.

Heat the remainder of the oil in a separate pan. Add the green bell pepper strips and sliced tomatoes and cook quickly over high heat for 2 to 3 minutes, remove from the pan and drain on paper towels.

To serve, sprinkle the baby corn jalfrezi with the garam masala and fresh cilantro and garnish with the pepper and tomato strips.

Khumbh palak

Spicy stir-fried mushrooms and spinach

This is a Kashmiri dish, which would be served as part of a main meal with rice and stuffed breads. I often serve this with Lamb in a pickled spice sauce (see page 74). They complement each other because one is mild and the other is hot.

Serves 4

3 tablespoons vegetable oil
1 teaspoon cumin seeds
¹/₂ teaspoon garlic pulp
1-inch piece fresh gingerroot, finely chopped
1 small green chili, finely chopped
1 cup chopped onions
¹/₂ teaspoon ground turmeric
9 ounces button mushrooms, wiped clean
2¹/₄ pounds spinach, washed and shredded
pinch of dried fenugreek leaves
1 tablespoon light cream
¹/₂ teaspoon garam masala
salt, to taste

Heat the oil in a karhai, wok, or large pan and add the cumin seeds. When they begin to crackle, stir in the garlic, ginger, green chili, onion, and turmeric. Add the mushrooms and cook, stirring, for 1 minute. Add the shredded spinach and cook over high heat for about 2 minutes, or until all the water evaporates.

Add the dried fenugreek leaves, cream, and garam masala and season.

Top right: **Spicy stir-fried mushrooms and spinach**
Right: **Baby corn jalfrezi**

Vattana nu saak
Green peas cooked with spices

This typically Gujarati dish was taught to me by my grandmother's cook.

Serves 4
2 tablespoons ghee or vegetable oil
1 teaspoon cumin seeds
¼ teaspoon white sesame seeds
5 cloves
2 cinnamon sticks
1 teaspoon black peppercorns, crushed
⅔ cup finely chopped onions
½ teaspoon ground turmeric
2 cups shelled peas, thawed if frozen
3 tablespoons chopped fresh cilantro
1 tablespoon chopped fresh mint
juice of ½ lemon
1 teaspoon sugar
salt, to taste
2 tablespoons grated fresh coconut

Heat the ghee or oil in a karhai, wok, or large skillet. Add the cumin seeds, white sesame seeds, cloves, cinnamon sticks, and crushed black pepper and stir-fry for 1 minute.

Add the chopped onions and cook for about 5 minutes until the onions begin to change color. Add the ground turmeric, peas, half of the chopped cilantro, the chopped mint, 1 cup water, and the lemon juice. Bring to a boil and simmer for about 10 minutes. Add the sugar and salt.

Sprinkle with grated coconut and the remaining chopped cilantro before serving.

◇ **My tip** For a slightly thicker sauce, puree about one-quarter of the peas in a food processor or blender and add to the pan with the rest of the peas.

Bhendi aur aloo masala subzi

Okra and potatoes

Okra is immensely popular in Gujarat, where this dish comes from. There are many ways of preparing okra, but this is one of my favorites. It is a dry dish, which works well as an accompaniment to a main dish, such as Chicken with fenugreek (see page 58) or with other vegetable dishes in a thali.

Serves 4

2 pounds small, tender okra
2 tablespoons vegetable oil
1 teaspoon cumin seeds
1½ cups peeled and diced potatoes
¼ teaspoon ground turmeric
2 tablespoons Cilantro, chili, garlic, and ginger paste (see page 20)
1 large tomato, chopped
salt, to taste
pinch of sugar
1 tablespoon lemon juice

Wash and wipe each okra with a dish towel (this prevents them going sticky when cooked). Cut the head and nip the end of each okra, then cut into 1-inch pieces.

Heat the oil in a large pan or wok and when nearly smoking hot, add the cumin seeds: These will start to crackle immediately. Add the potato dice, cover, and cook for 3 to 4 minutes, shaking the pan at regular intervals.

Stir in the ground turmeric and Cilantro, chili, garlic, and ginger paste and then the okra. Cover partially and cook over medium heat for 7 to 8 minutes. Stir in the chopped tomato and add the salt, sugar, and lemon juice. Cover and cook for 2 minutes longer. Serve hot.

◇ **My tip** This recipe can be completely altered by adding ¾ cup plain yogurt instead of the tomatoes and some extra salt and sugar. This will give the recipe a thick sauce.

Paneer chaman

Indian cheese in a mint and cilantro sauce

All paneer dishes originate in the north of India. This one comes from the eastern state of Bengal. Paneer is quite bland to taste and has a similar texture to tofu, but the beauty of it is that it takes on other flavors well. It is particularly good if browned first, as in this recipe.

Serves 4 to 6

vegetable oil for deep-frying
1¾ pounds paneer, diced
1½ cups roughly chopped fresh cilantro
1 teaspoon fresh mint, stems removed
1 ounce green chilies
1¼ cups plain yogurt
½ cup ghee
1½ teaspoons ajowan seeds
2 cups chopped onions
2 teaspoons ginger pulp
2 teaspoons garlic pulp
½ cup light cream
1 teaspoon East Indian garam masala (see page 23)
salt, to taste

Heat the oil in a large pan until it reaches a temperature of 375°F. Deep-fry the paneer until it turns golden brown. Remove from the oil and immerse in a bowl of cold water for 10 to 15 minutes; drain and set aside.

Place the fresh cilantro, mint, and green chilies in a food processor or blender and process,

Preparing okra

Above: **Indian cheese in a creamy tomato sauce**

Paneer makhni

Indian cheese in a creamy tomato sauce

This is a very typical dish in the Punjab region, where paneer is considered a very healthy source of protein. This is a light dish that can be eaten with chapattis or with Lentils with cream and butter (see page 106).

Serves 4 to 6
1¼ pounds chopped tomatoes
⅔ cup unsalted cashew nuts
2 tablespoons vegetable oil
7 tablespoons cream
1 cup plus 2 tablespoons butter
large pinch of dried fenugreek leaves
½ teaspoon ground white pepper
1¼ pounds paneer, cut into ½-inch cubes
salt, to taste
honey (optional)
light cream, to garnish

Place the tomatoes, cashew nuts, and oil in a large pan and bring to a boil. Simmer for 30 minutes, then leave to cool. Place the tomato and nut mixture in a food processor or blender and process to a fine puree.

Pass the puree through a strainer and return to the pan. Cook over medium heat and reduce by one-third, or until it becomes thick. Add the cream, butter, dried fenugreek, and white pepper and simmer for 10 to 15 minutes.

Add the paneer to the sauce and add salt. If the sauce is sour, add a little honey to sweeten. Garnish with cream and serve hot with a plain paratha (see page 99).

adding a little water to make a smooth paste. Whisk the yogurt in a bowl, add the Cilantro, mint, and chili paste and mix well.

Heat the ghee in a pan. Add the ajowan seeds and stir over medium heat for 10 seconds. Add the onions and cook, stirring, for 10 to 15 minutes until golden brown. Add the ginger and garlic and stir-fry for 1 minute. Add the mint and cilantro mixture and fry over medium heat until the oil begins to separate.

Add the fried paneer, stir-fry for 1 minute, then add the cream, garam masala, and salt. Increase the heat and leave to bubble for 1 minute and then serve.

◈ **My tip** For a slightly hotter dish, add ½ teaspoon cayenne pepper with the fresh green chilies.

Subzi curry

Mixed vegetable curry

"Subzi" is the generic term for vegetables and is recognized throughout India. I have used carrots, potatoes, and beans, but in India I would use whatever caught my eye at the market. Karela (bitter melon) is a wonderful Indian vegetable that you can use instead of the potatoes (see Preparing karela, below). You need to salt it before using to remove some of the moisture.

Serves 4
3 tablespoons ghee or vegetable oil
1 cup carrots, cut into batons
1 cup potatoes, peeled and cut into batons
3/4 cup green beans, cut into 1-inch
   pieces
4 bay leaves
1 onion, chopped
6 cloves garlic, crushed
2 green chilies, chopped
3/4 teaspoon cayenne pepper
1/2 teaspoon ground turmeric
1/2 teaspoon ground fennel
3/4 teaspoon ground cumin
2 teaspoons garam masala
salt, to taste
3 tablespoons chopped fresh cilantro

Heat half of the ghee or oil in a skillet. Add the carrots, potatoes, and green beans. Stir-fry for about 5 minutes; set aside.

Heat the remaining ghee or oil in a separate pan. Add the bay leaves and onion and cook, stirring, for 3 to 5 minutes. Add the garlic and green chilies and cook 3 minutes longer, stirring constantly.

Stir in the cayenne, ground turmeric, ground fennel, and cumin and cook for 1 minute. Add the carrots, potatoes, green beans, and about 2 cups water. Stir well and simmer for 5 to 10 minutes.

Add the garam masala and salt and simmer for another 5 minutes until the sauce thickens slightly. Serve hot, sprinkled with the chopped fresh cilantro.

Beans poriyal

Green beans with coconut

This dish is from southern India and is very quick to make—it is more of a stir-fry. I use fresh coconut in this recipe, but you could easily substitute the same amount of shredded coconut. It is delicious eaten with a fish curry and plain boiled rice.

Serves 4
3 tablespoons vegetable oil
1/2 teaspoon mustard seeds
2 dried red chilies
8 to 10 curry leaves
1/2 cup diced onion
1 green chili, chopped
21/2 cups green beans or snow peas, cut into
   1-inch pieces
salt, to taste
3/4 cup grated fresh coconut
juice of 1/2 lemon

Preparing karela

Heat the oil in a pan. When hot, add the mustard seeds, dried red chilies, and curry leaves. When the mustard seeds begin to crackle, add the diced onion and green chili. Increase the heat and stir-fry for 2 to 3 minutes.

Add the green beans and salt. Cook, covered, over low heat for 5 to 10 minutes until the beans are cooked, but not overdone. Add the grated coconut and lemon juice, mix well, and serve hot.

Left: **Green beans with coconut**

Baingan kalua
Sweet spicy eggplants

Eggplants are one of the most popular vegetables in Indian cooking, and especially in the Punjab, where this dish comes from. You can use the long white eggplants available from specialty markets—baby eggplants are also good. This is great as a side dish—perhaps served with an egg curry and a plain paratha or chapatti.

Serves 4
vegetable oil for deep-frying
1 pound eggplants, cut into 3/4-inch dice
3 tablespoons vegetable oil
1/2 teaspoon cumin seeds
1/2 teaspoon ground turmeric
1/4 teaspoon ground asafoetida
3/4 teaspoon cayenne pepper
2 teaspoons chopped fresh gingerroot
3/4 cup chickpea flour
4 teaspoons sugar
3/4 cup unsalted cashew nuts
salt, to taste

Deep-fry the eggplants in hot oil for 3 to 5 minutes until they change color and become tender. Remove from the oil with a slotted spoon and drain on paper towels.

In another pan, heat the 3 tablespoons oil, and add the cumin seeds. When they begin to crackle, add the turmeric, asafoetida, cayenne, and chopped ginger. Sprinkle with water and add the chickpea flour and sugar. Cook, stirring, for 3 to 5 minutes and then add the diced eggplants and cashew nuts. Add salt and sprinkle with more water if required.

Thali

The word "thali" actually refers to the plate that the food is served on, but has now come to mean a multidish meal. Originally invented in Gujarat, the thali is one of the most important contributions to Indian cuisine.

Usually made of stainless steel, and sometimes gold and silver, a thali is basically a large, round plate with several small bowls, called katoris. In southern India, a thali meal is often served on a large banana leaf. Most Gujaratis are vegetarian, so a traditional thali would consist of a number of vegetable dishes, both wet and dry, centered around a small mound of rice. Add some bread, a paneer (Indian cheese) dish, a dal, and some yogurt, plus, of course, the all-essential pickle or chutney, and you have a complete and balanced meal. The right-hand side of the dish is often reserved for the dessert, which would be served at the same time as all the other dishes. Silverware is never used—you eat a thali with your fingers.

The thali is a great way to experience Indian food and is served all over India and, increasingly, in Indian restaurants elsewhere. If you like the idea of being able to sample several small dishes, then this is a wonderful way of eating—often the only question you will be asked when ordering a thali in a restaurant is "vegetarian or non-vegetarian?" The rest is up to the cook who will prepare for you whatever is fresh and available.

Eating a thali for the first time can be daunting if you are not used to eating without a knife and fork. Indians are very deft with their hands when it comes to scooping up rice and vegetables with their fingers or using strips of bread to mop up the last of their dal. The best way to eat a thali is to get stuck in, eat and enjoy!

Many recipes in this book can be served as part of a thali. Try and balance different ingredients, as well as color and texture. Clockwise, from bottom: Cauliflower with ginger (page 80), Indian cheese in a mint and cilantro sauce (page 88), Mixed vegetable curry (page 90), Lentils with cream and butter (page 106), yogurt, Deep-fried puffed bread (page 102), and plain boiled rice.

Rice, bread, and accompaniments

Rice is the most important staple and has been cultivated in India for more than 3,000 years. There are numerous varieties—from long-grain white rice to the short red rice, eaten in rural areas in the south. Basmati is probably the most famous variety and I use it in all my cooking—it has an unmistakably sweet aroma and its name means "queen of fragrance." Although rice is eaten throughout India, it is more important to the southern diet, whereas the north of India relies more heavily on wheat. Bread is served with almost every meal—from the familiar chapatti to the delicious puri, a snack bread that puffs up when deep-fried. Dals, or dishes made from lentils and legumes, are eaten all over India, although the type of legumes used and methods of cooking vary enormously from region to region, so there are countless variations on the theme. I have included some of my favorite dal recipes here, from Chickpea curry (see page 105) to South Indian lentil curry (see page 106). No Indian meal is complete without relishes and chutneys. Some are exceedingly hot while others, such as raita, are designed to cool down a hot dish.

Above: **Rice growing in the paddy fields of southern India.** *Opposite:* **Local girls working at a pappadum factory in Chennai.**

Tayir sadam
Yogurt with rice

I have had this dish so often, but it still remains one of my favorites. My grandmother used to pack me off to school with this in my tiffin, and for me it is everything that home cooking should be. It is the one dish I crave when I feel under the weather.

Serves 4

2¼ cups basmati rice, cooked
½ cup plain yogurt
salt, to taste
½ teaspoon ginger pulp
½ teaspoon chopped green chili
1 tablespoon vegetable oil
¼ teaspoon mustard seeds
¼ teaspoon skinned split black
   lentils (urad dal)
6 curry leaves
2 dried red chilies, seeded
½ teaspoon ground asafoetida
1 tablespoon chopped fresh
   cilantro, to garnish

Place the cooked rice in a large bowl and mash with a masher, adding a little cold water to prevent it sticking.

   Add the yogurt and salt and mix well. Stir in the ginger and chopped green chili.

   Heat the oil. When hot, add the mustard seeds, lentils, curry leaves, and dried red chilies. When the mustard seeds start to crackle, stir in the asafoetida and then pour over the rice and serve, garnished with the chopped fresh cilantro.

Jeera pulav

Rice flavored with cumin seeds

This is a wonderfully simple rice dish that would be eaten every day in most Indian households—it is also very simple to make. I certainly prefer it to plain boiled rice. The cumin seeds complement the fragrant basmati rice perfectly.

Serves 4

1¼ cups basmati rice
1½ tablespoons vegetable oil
2 cloves
2 cardamom pods
1 bay leaf
1 teaspoon cumin seeds
½ teaspoon salt

Wash the rice in several changes of water and then leave to soak in a large bowl of cold water.

In a karhai, wok, or large pan, heat the oil. Add the cloves, cardamom pods, bay leaf, and cumin seeds. When the cumin seeds begin to crackle, drain the rice and add to the pan.

Fry over low heat until the oil coats the rice grains.

Add the salt and pour in 2½ cups water, stir lightly so the rice does not stick to the bottom of the pan. Bring to a boil and then reduce the heat and simmer, covered, for 10 minutes until the water has been absorbed and the rice is cooked.

If the rice is cooked and the water is not completely absorbed, remove the lid to leave the water to evaporate.

◇ **My tip** To make perfect rice, wash 2 cups of basmati rice in several changes of warm water; set aside for 20 minutes in a colander. Bring the rice and 1 quart hot water to a boil in a pan; stir gently. Cover and simmer for 10 minutes until all the water has been absorbed.

Opposite: **Yogurt with rice, South Indian Lentil curry, and Black pepper chicken**

Khakhra

Crispy Gujarati bread

Although this is called "bread," it is actually more like a cracker that is eaten with tea as a snack. Whenever I go back to India, I almost certainly snack on a few of these!

Makes 8

⅔ cup wholewheat flour, sifted
⅔ cup all-purpose flour, sifted
½ teaspoon salt
1 teaspoon garam masala
1 tablespoon vegetable oil
7 tablespoons milk or warm water
4 tablespoons ghee

In a bowl, mix together the flours, salt, and garam masala. Add the oil and rub in. Add the milk or water and knead to make a soft dough. Divide the dough into 8 equal parts and then roll out each into a thin circle.

Heat a griddle pan and cook the bread one at a time, turning once, for a few minutes each side. As you cook each one, brush with a little ghee and pile them up.

Return the pile of breads to the griddle and, using a clean folded dish towel, press down and continue to cook on the griddle. Turn them over and repeat on the other side. This prevents the breads from puffing up.

◇ **My tip** I find these breads can be kept in airtight containers for up to 2 weeks.

Chapatti

Indian flat bread

Chapattis are eaten all over India as an accompaniment to most meals—they really are a national bread. The art is in the shaping—a good chapatti should be perfectly round. When I am away from home on my travels the one thing my husband Kirit complains about is that he doesn't get his fresh homemade chapattis.

Makes 10

1½ cups wholewheat flour, sifted
½ teaspoon salt (optional)
1 tablespoon vegetable oil
melted ghee or butter

Mix the flour, salt, and ⅔ cup water in a bowl. Add the oil and knead to a soft dough; leave covered with a wet cloth for 30 minutes.

Knead the dough again for 10 minutes, then divide into 10 pieces using a little flour to shape them into round balls. Press out each piece on a floured board using your fingers. Roll out with a rolling pin into thin pancakes 4 to 5 inches in diameter.

Heat a flat skillet or hot griddle. Cook each chapatti over medium heat for 30 seconds, and when one side dries up and tiny bubbles begin to appear, turn it over and cook until brown spots appear on the under surface. Press the sides down gently with a clean dish towel.

Remove from the griddle with a pair of tongs and place directly over the heat/flame until it puffs up. Smear one side with a little ghee or butter and serve immediately.

Paratha

Flaky bread

Parathas originated in the north of India, where wheat is a staple. I love to eat these delicious flaky breads for breakfast.

Makes 6
1¹/₂ cups wholewheat flour, sifted
¹/₂ teaspoon salt
1 tablespoon vegetable oil
6 tablespoons ghee or butter, melted
extra flour for dusting

Put the flour, salt, and ²/₃ cup water in a bowl and knead to a soft dough. Mix in the oil and set aside, covered, for 30 minutes.

Divide the dough into 6 equal parts and shape into round balls. Flatten and roll out into flat disks about 5 inches in diameter.

Smear a little ghee on to the paratha (upper surface only) and fold it over into a semicircle. Smear more ghee over the upper surface and fold it again to form a triangle shape. Place on a floured board and roll into a thin triangle, making sure the edges are not thick.

Place on a hot griddle. Cook for 1 minute, then turn over. When the paratha begins to color, brush a little ghee on one side. Turn over and cook. Brush a little ghee on this side also.

Cook for a few seconds longer until the paratha is golden brown on both sides.

Serve hot.

◇ **My tip** For a quick sweet snack, I like to sprinkle a little brown sugar on top of my chapatti and lightly broil it for a few minutes until the sugar caramelizes. You can also add a sliced banana with the sugar and serve with cream.

Roomali roti

Handkerchief-thin bread

Roomali roti is eaten mainly in the north of India. Roomali means "handkerchief"—the dough is rolled out until it is paper thin and then cooked over an upturned karhai. It is a little fiddly to make but the end result is truly worth it.

Makes 6
1 cup plus 2 tablespoons all-purpose flour, sifted
¹/₃ cup wholewheat flour, sifted
1 teaspoon salt
1 teaspoon sugar
2 tablespoons melted ghee or vegetable oil
1 egg
milk or water for kneading

Place the flours, salt, and sugar in a bowl. Rub in the ghee or oil. Break in the egg and slowly add the milk or water to form a soft dough. Keep covered for 30 minutes: The dough should be very smooth and elastic. Shape into 6 balls and roll out evenly so they are as thin as tissue paper.

Heat an upturned karhai over a gas flame and cook each roti on the curved base of the pan for 1 minute. Fold like a handkerchief and serve.

◇ **My tip** Making this roti requires a little practice. Start by making a good elastic dough, which can be rolled out very thinly.

Methi thepla

Chickpea flour pancakes with fenugreek

This dish is originally part of a staple diet eaten by Gujarati farmers and taken out into the fields. It is best when accompanied by plain yogurt and sliced onions. I like to reheat any leftover pancakes and eat them with ginger tea. The chilies are optional in this recipe. If you don't want hot pancakes, simply leave them out.

Makes 8

3/4 cup plus 2 tablespoons chickpea flour, sifted
2/3 cup all-purpose flour, sifted
1 teaspoon ground cumin
1/4 teaspoon ground asafoetida
1/2 teaspoon ground turmeric
1/2 teaspoon salt
1 teaspoon grated fresh ginger root
1 small green chili, chopped (optional)
1 tablespoon finely chopped fresh cilantro
2 ounces fresh fenugreek, finely chopped
1 tablespoon vegetable oil
ghee or butter, to smear

Place the sifted flours, ground cumin, asafoetida, ground turmeric, and salt in a bowl. Add the grated ginger, green chili, if using, fresh cilantro, and fenugreek. Add enough water to make a soft dough and then mix in the oil; set aside for 10 minutes.

Divide the dough into 8 equal portions and roll out into disks about 4 inches in diameter.

Pour a little oil or ghee onto a hot griddle. Cook the pancakes for about 1 minute and then turn over and cook the other side until brown specks appear on the surface. Brush with ghee or butter then remove after a few more seconds and serve.

◇ **My tip** I sometimes add 1/2 teaspoon sesame seeds to the mixture. As an alternative, you can also use 4 ounces grated pumpkin or doodhi (see page 108), instead of the fenugreek leaves. Take care to squeeze out any excess moisture before adding it to the flour or the dough will become too wet.

Uttappam

Flat rice bread from Southern India

Although I call this a bread, it is actually more like a thick, round pancake, eaten as a snack. The fresh chilies, tomatoes, and cilantro add color and a fresh taste. You can seed the chilies if you want less heat.

Makes 8

generous 1 cup basmati rice
½ cup white lentils
salt, to taste
1 teaspoon sugar
½ teaspoon baking soda
1 cup chopped onions
1 cup skinned, seeded and diced tomatoes
1 green chili, chopped
½ cup chopped fresh cilantro
ghee or vegetable oil, as desired

Wash the rice and lentils separately in several changes of water. Leave each to soak in a large pan of clean water for a couple of hours.

Drain the rice and place in a food processor or blender and grind to a smooth paste. Add a little water to form a thick batter. Do the same with the lentils.

Add the salt, sugar, and baking soda to the rice batter and mix well. Stir in the white lentil batter. Mix well and set aside to ferment for at least 12 to 15 hours.

Place the chopped onion, diced tomatoes, chopped green chili, and chopped cilantro in separate bowls.

Heat a griddle or nonstick pan. Brush with a little ghee or oil and pour in 2 to 3 tablespoons of the batter. Spread evenly with the back of a spoon into a thick circle 4 inches in diameter.

Garnish the surface with a little of each of the onion, tomato, green chili, and chopped cilantro and spread evenly. Sprinkle some oil or ghee over and around the bread. Cook over low heat until small bubbles appear on the surface, about 5 minutes.

Turn over and cook the other side until crisp and golden. Alternatively, you can finish it off under a hot broiler for 1 to 2 minutes. Serve hot with South Indian lentil curry (see page 106).

Khasta roti

Indian puffed bread

This superb, soft bread is not really an everyday bread—it is something you would make only on special occasions. It is a little time-consuming to make, but if you offer this to your guests, they will love it and know that you have gone to a lot of trouble to please them.

Makes 6

1½ **cups wholewheat flour, sifted**
1 **teaspoon baking powder**
½ **teaspoon salt**
½ **cup ghee, melted**
1½ **teaspoons cumin seeds**
7 **tablespoons milk**
2 **eggs, beaten**

Mix together the flour, baking powder, salt, ghee, and cumin seeds in a bowl. Mix well, rubbing the ghee into the flour. Make into a dough by mixing in the milk and the beaten eggs; set aside, covered, for 20 minutes.

Divide the dough into 6 equal parts and shape into round balls. Roll out each of the rounds into a flat cake about 5 inches in diameter.

Cook over a hot griddle for 1 minute on one side and then turn over; cook for another minute. Continue cooking on both sides by turning over frequently until cooked, 5 to 10 minutes. Serve immediately while still crisp and hot.

Sada puri

Deep-fried puffed bread

Puris are delicious disks of dough that puff up when deep-fried (see below). They are often eaten as snacks or as accompaniments to meat or vegetable dishes. They are also great fun to make and children love seeing the dough circles puff up as they cook.

Makes 20

1½ **cups wholewheat flour, sifted**
1 **teaspoon salt**
4 **tablespoons semolina**
1½ **tablespoons vegetable oil or melted ghee**
vegetable oil for deep-frying

Place the flour, salt, and semolina in a bowl. Warm the oil or ghee and rub into the flour. Adding a little water at a time, knead to make a stiff dough. Cover with a damp cloth and set aside for 30 minutes.

Knead the dough again and divide into 20 equal portions. Shape into balls in the palm of your hand and roll out on a floured surface into circles of 3 to 3½ inches in diameter.

Heat the vegetable oil in a large heavy-bottomed pan. When the temperature reaches 375°F, fry the puris one at a time. Gently push them into the oil with a slotted spoon. When they puff up (almost immediately), turn over, and cook on the other side.

Remove from the pan with a slotted spoon and drain on paper towels.

Frying Sada puri

Palak puri

Deep-fried spinach bread

This is very similar to Sada puri (see opposite), but has pureed spinach added to the dough, giving it a wonderful greenish color.

Makes 20
2 ounces fresh spinach leaves, washed
1/4 ounce fresh gingerroot
1/2 cups wholewheat flour, sifted
1/2 teaspoon salt
1/2 teaspoon cayenne pepper
2 tablespoons ghee
1 teaspoon cumin seeds
vegetable oil for deep-frying

Blanch the spinach leaves in boiling water, refresh in cold water, and drain again. Place in a food processor or blender with the ginger and grind to a fine paste.

Sift together the flour, salt, and cayenne and then rub in the ghee. Add the spinach and ginger paste and the cumin seeds and mix well. Add enough water and knead well to form a soft dough; set aside for 15 minutes.

Knead again and divide into 20 equal parts. Shape into round balls and then flatten into round disks 3 inches in diameter.

Heat the vegetable oil in a large heavy-bottomed pan until the temperature reaches 375°F. Reduce the heat to very low and fry the puris one at a time so they "puff up."

Remove with a slotted spoon and drain on paper towels.

Gajjar ki roti

Carrot bread

Carrots are a wonderfully versatile vegetable—they can be made into soups, curries, desserts, and a delicious bread, as here. I like to eat this bread with plain yogurt for a snack.

Makes 8

1½ cups wholewheat flour, plus
   extra for dusting
½ teaspoon salt
⅔ cup grated carrots
1 tablespoon vegetable oil
ghee or butter for spreading

Sift the flour and salt into a large bowl and add the grated carrots. Add ½ to ⅔ cup water and knead to make a soft dough. Add the oil and mix well; set aside for 1 hour.

Divide the dough into 8 pieces and shape into balls. Flatten each piece with the palm of your hand and then roll out into a thin pancake approximately 5 inches in diameter.

Heat a griddle or flat pan and cook the rotis over medium heat for 45 seconds. When bubbles appear on the surface, turn it over and cook until brown spots appear on the under surface.

Turn over and repeat the process until all the rotis are well cooked— about 5 minutes. Remove from the heat and smear both sides with ghee or butter. Serve hot.

Punjabi chole

Chickpea curry

This is a dish in the Punjab. It would be eaten with bread, such as Deep-fried spinach bread (see page 103) or Flaky bread (see page 99), as a simple brunch dish or with a lamb or tandoori chicken dish as part of a main meal.

Serves 4 to 6

1¹/₂ cups dried chickpeas, or 1 can (7-ounces), drained
1 tablespoon ground coriander
2 teaspoons ground fennel
³/₄ teaspoon ground amchoor
1 teaspoon ground cumin
¹/₂ teaspoon ground turmeric
¹/₂ teaspoon chat masala
³/₄ teaspoon crushed black peppercorns
²/₃ cup melted ghee
¹/₂ ounce green chili juliennes
¹/₂ ounce ginger juliennes
3 tablespoons chopped fresh cilantro
2 tablespoons chopped fresh mint
salt, to taste

If using dried chickpeas, soak them overnight in water. Place in a large pan of salted water and bring to a boil. Cover and cook until soft, about 30 minutes, and then drain.

Mix together all the ground spices and crushed black peppercorns. Place half the freshly cooked or canned chickpeas in a pan and sprinkle with half the spice mix. Heat the ghee until it is very hot and then pour half the hot ghee over the chickpeas.

Sprinkle with half of the green chili, ginger, cilantro, and mint. Add the remaining chickpeas followed by the remainder of the spice mix, chili, ginger, cilantro, and mint. Finish with the rest of the hot ghee and mix well. Add salt and serve immediately.

Left: **Chickpea curry and Deep-fried spinach bread served with a fresh tomato and red onion salad.**

Sambhar

South Indian lentil curry

This is a very common staple dish from the south of India, where it would be served with rice. It makes a great accompaniment to a main dish and goes well with Flat rice bread (see page 99).

Serves 4
5 tablespoons vegetable oil
3 dried red chilies
5 teaspoons coriander seeds
1/2 teaspoon fenugreek seeds
4 tablespoons grated fresh coconut
3/4 cup yellow lentils (toover dal)
1/2 teaspoon ground turmeric
1/2 cup sliced onions
1/4 teaspoon ground asafoetida
1/2 cup diced tomatoes
1 cup diced eggplant
3/4 ounce tamarind pulp
salt, to taste
1/2 teaspoon sugar
8 curry leaves
1/2 teaspoon mustard seeds

Heat half the oil in a pan and add the red chilies, coriander seeds, fenugreek seeds, and grated coconut. Cook, stirring, for 5 to 10 minutes; set aside to cool.

Wash the yellow lentils in several changes of water and place in a large pan of water. Bring to a boil, add the ground turmeric, and simmer for 15 to 20 minutes.

Put the coconut, chili, and spice mix in a food processor or blender and process to a fine paste.

When the lentils are soft and mushy add the sliced onions, asafoetida, diced tomatoes, diced eggplant, and coconut paste and continue to cook for 5 minutes. Add the tamarind pulp, salt, and sugar and simmer for 2 minutes longer.

Heat the remaining oil in a separate pan and add the curry leaves and mustard seeds. When they begin to crackle, pour them over the lentils and serve immediately with plain boiled rice.

Dal makhni

Lentils with cream and butter

This is a very typical Punjabi dish containing a lot of cream and butter. Don't let the calories put you off—this wonderfully warming dish is very nutritious and high in protein. If you do want a healthier version, use oil instead of butter. I could eat this with just about anything, but it is simply delicious with just rice and parathas.

Serves 4
3 cloves garlic
1 teaspoon green cardamom pods
1 teaspoon cloves
1 cinnamon stick
2 teaspoons cumin seeds
3/4 cup black lentils (urad dal)
1/4 cup red kidney beans
1 cup light cream
14 tablespoons (13/4 sticks) butter, or 3 tablespoons vegetable oil
1/2 teaspoon cayenne pepper
salt, to taste
chopped fresh cilantro, to garnish

Using a mortar and pestle, roughly crush together the garlic, cardamom pods, cloves, cinnamon, and cumin seeds. Tie up this mixture in a 3-inch square piece of cheesecloth to form a "bouquet garni," and place in a large pan with the black lentils and red kidney beans. Add enough water to cover the legumes and bring to a boil. Boil for 10 minutes. Reduce the heat and simmer gently for about 1 hour, adding more water if necessary.

When the legumes are cooked and the mixture has thickened, remove the "bouquet garni," and discard. Add the cream, butter or oil, cayenne, and salt. Sprinkle with a little chopped fresh cilantro to serve.

Opposite: **Lentils with cream and butter**

Dal triveni

Three-lentil dal

There are three types of lentils in this dish—
toover, channa, and masoor—hence its name,
triveni, meaning "three." It is a very simple
recipe but is absolutely delicious eaten with pilau
rice and Chickpea flour pancakes with fenugreek
(see page 100). The asafoetida helps to
counteract the sometimes negative side effects of
eating lentils in large quantities!

Serves 4

⅓ cup yellow lentils (toover dal)
⅓ cup split yellow peas (channa dal)
⅓ cup split red lentils (masoor dal)
5 tablespoons vegetable oil
1 teaspoon cumin seeds
½ teaspoon mustard seeds
¼ teaspoon ground asafoetida
½ teaspoon ground turmeric
½ teaspoon cayenne pepper
2-inch piece fresh gingerroot, cut into juliennes
1 small green chili, cut into juliennes
1 small tomato, skinned, seeded and diced
2 tablespoons chopped fresh cilantro, to garnish

Wash the three different dals together in several
changes of water. Place in a large heavy-
bottomed pan and cover with cold water. Bring
to a boil and simmer for about 40 minutes until
they are soft and cooked; set aside.

Heat the oil in another pan and add the cumin
seeds and mustard seeds. When they begin to
crackle, add the asafoetida, turmeric, and
cayenne. Stir in the ginger, green chili, and diced
tomato and cook for 1 minute.

Add the mixture to the boiling lentils and stir
well. Sprinkle with chopped fresh cilantro and
serve.

Doodhi chana dal

Pumpkin and chickpeas

This is a typical dish from Gujarat and is a staple
food for farmers in that region. There are many
types of pumpkin, but the ones available in the
Indian grocery stores are called "lauki" or
"doodhi." This dish is absolutely delicious
eaten plain with chapattis.

Serves 4

1 pound pumpkin
2 tablespoons vegetable oil
1 teaspoon black mustard seeds
pinch of asafoetida
1 teaspoon sugar
1 onion, sliced
2½ cups dried chickpeas, soaked
3 tablespoons canned chopped tomatoes with juice
2 tablespoons Cilantro, chili, garlic, and ginger
    paste (see page 20)
¼ teaspoon ground turmeric
salt, to taste
chopped fresh cilantro, to garnish

Peel the pumpkin and cut into 2-inch cubes; soak
in water (if not using immediately).

Heat the oil in a large heavy-bottomed pan
and add the mustard seeds. When they start to
"pop," add the asafoetida, sugar, and onion and
cook until the onion browns slightly. Add the
chickpeas and tomatoes, cover, and cook for
about 10 minutes.

Add the Cilantro, chili, garlic, and ginger
paste, ground turmeric, pumpkin, and ⅔ cup
water, cover and cook for 5 to 7 minutes longer.

Serve hot with rice or bread.

Preparing doodhi

Begum ka salat

Princess salad

This delightful salad is made in many north Indian households where there is a large Muslim population—the word "begum" is the Urdu word for "princess," and is often used to describe the lady of the house. It is great as a side dish but you could also serve it as an appetizer with bread.

Serves 4

1/2 cup yellow split peas (channa dal)
14 ounces potatoes, peeled
1 pomegranate (see My tip)
4 tablespoons lemon juice
1 tablespoon chat masala
3 tablespoons vegetable oil
1 tablespoon sugar
pinch of baking soda
salt, to taste
1 cup red onion, sliced into rings
2 tablespoons chopped fresh mint

Soak the split peas in cold water overnight. Drain and place in a large pan with enough salted water to cover. Bring to a boil and simmer for about 20 minutes until soft, but not mushy. In another pan, boil the potatoes until tender; leave to cool and then cut into small dice.

Halve the pomegranate and pick out the seeds with a fork; rinse the seeds and drain. In a bowl, combine the potatoes, split peas, pomegranate seeds, lemon juice, chat masala, vegetable oil, sugar, baking soda, and salt and set aside for 30 minutes for the flavors to infuse.

Serve garnished with red onion slices and chopped fresh mint.

◇ **My tip** You need only the seeds from the pomegranate for this recipe, but keep the juice—it is delicious. Be careful when preparing pomegranate—the juice will stain clothes.

Dhaniya pudhina raita

Cilantro and mint raita

This lovely bright green raita is delicious as a dip for pappadums, samosas, or pakoras. It is also wonderful with kabobs. In an Indian household it would be made fresh every day, but you can store it for up to a week in the refrigerator.

Serves 4

5 ounces fresh cilantro
2 ounces fresh mint
1 green chili, chopped
4 cloves garlic, crushed
juice of ¹/₂ lime
1 cup thick plain yogurt
¹/₂ teaspoon sugar
salt, to taste

Place the fresh cilantro, fresh mint, green chili, and garlic in a food processor or blender and process to a fine paste. Add the lime juice and a little water, if required.

Place the yogurt in a glass bowl and whisk in the green paste. Add the sugar and salt.

You can also make it in advance by freezing the paste before you add the yogurt.

Safarchand chutney

Apple relish

Apples are not a traditionally Indian ingredient but, combined with sugar and aromatic spices, they make a delicious sweet and tangy chutney, perfect as a dip for snacks.

Serves 4

1¹/₄ pounds cooking apples, peeled, cored, and diced
2 cloves
2 cardamom pods
1 bay leaf
1¹/₂ cups sugar
a few saffron strands
salt, to taste
1¹/₂ teaspoons ground cumin

Put the apples in a large pan with 1 cup water.

Tie the cloves, cardamom pods, and bay leaf in a 3-inch square piece of cheesecloth to form a "bouquet garni." Add to the pan with the sugar and saffron. Cook over low heat for about 30 minutes, or until the apples become soft and mushy.

Leave to cool, remove the "bouquet garni," and then pass through a fine strainer. Add the salt and ground cumin. Store in an airtight container in the refrigerator for up to 2 weeks.

Preparing coconut

Imli chutney

Tamarind and date chutney

This is a really delicious chutney, which is perfect for serving with hot snacks, such as vegetable samosas.

Serves 4

5 ounces tamarind pulp
7 ounces dates
1/3 cup soft light brown sugar
4 teaspoons cumin seeds, roasted and ground
1/2 teaspoon cayenne pepper
1/2 teaspoon black salt (optional)
salt, to taste

Place the tamarind pulp, dates, brown sugar, and 1³/₄ cups water in a pan and bring to a boil. Cook for 25 to 30 minutes, stirring occasionally.

Remove from the heat and leave to cool. Place in a food processor or blender and puree to a smooth consistency, making sure there are no seeds in the tamarind pulp; pass through a fine strainer.

Add the roasted cumin and cayenne, and black salt, if using. Taste and adjust the seasoning. Store in an airtight container in the refrigerator for up to 2 weeks.

Subzi raita

Mixed vegetable raita

This fresh tasting raita is a classic accompaniment to biryani dishes.

Serves 4

1¹/₄ cups plain yogurt
1¹/₂ teaspoons sugar
salt, to taste
1 teaspoon cumin seeds, roasted and ground
1/2 cup chopped onions
1/2 cup finely diced tomatoes
1/2 cup cucumber, seeded and chopped
1 tablespoon chopped fresh cilantro

Combine the yogurt and sugar together with a whisk. Stir in salt and the ground roasted cumin.

Add the onions, tomatoes, and cucumber and serve garnished with chopped cilantro.

Thengai pachadi

Coconut and yogurt dip

This refreshing and cooling dip comes from Kerala, where coconuts are used in some form or other in a wide range of dishes.

Serves 4 to 6

3 cups grated fresh coconut
2 green chilies
³/₄ ounce fresh gingerroot, grated
1 tablespoon chopped fresh cilantro
2¹/₄ cups plain yogurt
salt, to taste
1¹/₂ tablespoons vegetable oil
1/2 teaspoon mustard seeds
8 to 10 curry leaves

Place the coconut, green chilies, ginger, and cilantro in a food processor or blender and grind to a smooth paste. Add the yogurt, mix well, and add the salt.

Heat the oil in a pan and add the mustard seeds. When they start to crackle, add the curry leaves, and then pour into the coconut mixture; mix well. Serve chilled as a dip for snacks.

Desserts and drinks

Because of the abundance of delicious fresh fruit grown in India, it is more usual to finish a meal with a piece of fresh mango, banana, or melon, depending on the season. However, Indians are famous for having an incredibly sweet tooth and have devised all manner of sweets and desserts, often milk-based, to satisfy their sugar cravings. As well as milk, yogurt features in many Indian desserts, along with nuts, dried fruits, saffron, coconut, and, of course, sugar. Indians can be very inventive, and sweet puddings are also made from ingredients such as carrots and peas. Desserts are not really made or served every day, but are reserved for special occasions such as religious festivals or weddings. Diwali is just such an occasion and is certainly a time when you would offer sweets, often decorated with edible gold or silver leaf.

Cooling drinks are very popular in India, particularly in the north in the scorching summer months. A yogurt lassi is just the thing to cool you down—yogurt is excellent for reducing body temperature, as well as settling the stomach. Some drinks are welcome drinks, others are best drunk after a meal, but all of them are delicious and refreshing—enjoy!

Above and opposite: **Selecting fruit in Kerala. Mangoes, limes, coconuts, and bananas are everywhere in abundance.**

Shrikhand

Creamy saffron yogurt

In my grandmother's house in India we would make fresh plain yogurt every day, but this recipe works just as well with bought yogurt.

Serves 4 to 6

5 cups plain yogurt

5 tablespoons milk

a few saffron strands

1/2 cup sugar

1 teaspoon ground cardamom

1 teaspoon pistachio slivers

MANGOES

Mangoes are probably my favorite fruit. If I'm ever in India during the mango season I go mad for them, eating them at every meal, in milkshakes and ice cream, but more often just on their own. There are hundreds of varieties, but the king of mangoes is the alphonso, which is grown in Maharashtra, where I grew up. I remember pickling mangoes at my grandmother's house—it was a great excuse for a family get-together and was often the cause for lots of excitement. My grandmother, of course, was the only one who knew the secret spice blend—the rest of us were just helpers following her instructions. After a few days the job would be finished and all the various pickles and chutneys would be stored away in huge earthenware jars to last us the year until the next mango season.

Pour the yogurt onto a clean, very fine piece of cheesecloth and bring together the 4 corners of the cloth. Tie a tight knot and hang overnight over a sink, undisturbed, until all the whey has drained out.

Place the milk in a small pan and add the saffron strands. Bring slowly to a boil and then remove from the heat. Set aside so the milk is infused with the saffron and turns a pale yellow color.

Empty the contents of the cloth carefully into a bowl and whisk in the sugar until it dissolves. Add the saffron milk and ground cardamom and mix well.

Pour into small serving dishes and serve chilled, garnished with pistachio slivers.

Kesari phirnee

Ground rice pudding with saffron milk

This delicately scented dessert comes from Gujarat. It is traditionally served in earthenware pots (see opposite). The yellow color comes from the saffron.

Serves 4 to 6

1 1/4 cups fresh whole milk

1/4 cup sugar

a few saffron strands

5 tablespoons rice flour

2 tablespoons ground blanched almonds

1 can (14-oz) condensed milk

1 teaspoon ground cardamom

1 tablespoon roughly chopped pistachio nuts

Place the whole milk in a heavy-bottomed pan and bring to a boil. Add the sugar and saffron strands and stir well over low heat.

Sprinkle the rice flour and ground almonds over and whisk vigorously until the mixture begins to thicken. Add the condensed milk and stir well. Cook for 2 to 3 minutes longer.

Stir in the ground cardamom and serve in small dishes garnished with pistachio nuts.

Opposite: **Ground rice pudding with saffron milk**

Shahi tukra

Fried bread steeped in milk

This dessert is very popular in the north of India and was first introduced in the royal kitchens. The saffron and pistachios, both prized ingredients, mean that it is a dessert that is associated with special occasions.

Serves 4
4 slices of white bread
vegetable oil for frying
1 cup milk
a few saffron strands
1 cup sugar
few drops of vanilla extract
4 teaspoons pistachio slivers

Remove the crusts from the bread and fry the bread in oil until golden brown. Remove from the pan, drain on paper towels, then arrange in a shallow serving dish.

Place the milk in a heavy-bottomed pan and add the saffron strands. Bring slowly to a boil. Pour the milk over the bread and leave to soak in.

Place the sugar and vanilla in a separate pan with about 7 tablespoons water. Bring to a boil, stirring all the time and pour over the bread and milk.

Leave to cool, then serve sprinkled with pistachio slivers.

Ghee gol rotli

Sweetened bread and butter

Indians love sweet food, and this is a delicious snack as well as a dessert. It does have a high calorie content, but when I was a child my grandmother was of the opinion that children needed plenty of sugar to give them energy. This became one of my favorites.

Serves 4
6 tablespoons ghee
4 heaped tablespoons jaggery
pinch of grated nutmeg
¼ teaspoon ground cardamom
8 chapattis (see below)

In a bowl, mix the ghee, jaggery, nutmeg, and ground cardamom. Warm the chapattis slightly.

Spread a little of the mixture evenly on one side of a chapatti and then roll up into a cylindrical wrap. Repeat with the other chapattis and serve immediately.

◇ **My tip** Chapattis are available in some large supermarkets and Indian grocery stores, as well as some natural-food stores. However, if you want to make your own, see the recipe on page 98.

Rabadi

Strawberry milk dessert

Rabadi means "reduced milk" and milk-based desserts and sweets are popular all over India. This is one of my favorites—I do not need an excuse to make this dessert and will often eat it as a snack.

Serves 4
2 quarts full-fat milk
1³/₄ cups sugar
¹/₂ cup strawberry puree
5 ounces chopped strawberries
strawberry slices, to garnish

Place the milk in a heavy-bottomed pan and slowly bring to a boil. Reduce the heat and cook for about 20 minutes, stirring constantly. Continue to heat the milk, stirring every 5 minutes, until the milk is reduced to 1 quart and has the consistency of thick cream: This should take about 1¹/₂ to 2 hours.

Remove the pan from the heat, add the sugar, and stir until dissolved. Add the strawberry puree and chopped strawberries.

Leave to cool, then serve in shallow dishes, garnished with a few strawberry slices.

Matar ki kheer

Cardamom and pea pudding

Peas are not normally associated with desserts, but I find that they work really well here. I invented this dish when I once had to prepare a dish for some guests at short notice.

Serves 4

2 cups shelled peas, thawed if frozen
2 tablespoons ghee
2 tablespoons roughly chopped cashew nuts
2 tablespoons raisins
1¹/₂ quarts milk
1³/₄ cups plus 2 tablespoons sugar
¹/₂ teaspoon ground cardamom or a few drops of
vanilla extract
light cream, to decorate

Place the peas in a pan with water to cover and boil for about 5 minutes; refresh in cold water and drain again. Place in a food processor or blender and process to a smooth paste.

Heat the ghee in a heavy-bottomed pan. Add the cashew nuts and raisins and fry for 1 minute. Add the green pea paste and cook for a few minutes, stirring constantly.

Add the milk and sugar and bring to a boil. Cook over low heat for 15 to 20 minutes, or until the milk has reduced by half. Add the ground cardamom or vanilla extract and cook for another 5 minutes; remove from the heat and leave to cool slightly.

Pour into serving dishes and serve chilled, decorated with a swirl of cream.

Bibinca

Coconut milk layered cake

This dessert is an essential part of the Christmas festivities on the west coast, particularly Goa. The number of layers is important—the more layers, the more effort your host has gone to.

Serves 4

1 cup plus 2 tablespoons white or brown sugar
5 cardamom pods, crushed
1 cup all-purpose flour
5 egg yolks
1 cup coconut milk
few drops of vanilla extract
¹/₂ cup (1 stick) unsalted butter or ghee, melted

Place the sugar in 1 cup water in a heavy-bottomed pan and heat slowly to dissolve the sugar. Add the cardamom pods and continue to heat for 10 minutes. Strain to remove the cardamom pods and set aside to cool.

Combine the flour, egg yolks, coconut milk, and cooled sugar syrup in another bowl. Whisk well to make a smooth, flowing batter, making sure there are not any lumps. Add the vanilla extract, mix well, and set aside for approximately 45 minutes.

Preheat a broiler. Take a 6- to 8-inch crêpe pan (preferably nonstick) and set it over medium heat. When it is hot, add about ¹/₂ cup of the batter to the pan using a ladle and spread it evenly onto the pan by tilting it in all directions.

Cook over low to medium heat until the top and bottom are golden brown. Add another ¹/₂ cup batter on top of the first layer and spread out. Broil until the second layer is golden brown; continue until all the batter is used.

Leave to cool before turning out of the pan. Cut into tiny wedges and serve.

Lassi

Chilled yogurt drink

Drinking lassi is a great way to beat the heat of the scorching sun in summer. Yogurt has many health-giving properties and this drink is perfect for settling the stomach—particularly after a very spicy Indian meal. It can be served sweet or salted.

Serves 4

1³/₄ cups plain yogurt
¹/₃ cup sugar, or 1¹/₂ teaspoons salt
1 teaspoon roasted coriander seeds, crushed
pistachio slivers, to garnish

Pour the yogurt into a bowl, add the sugar or salt and slightly less than 1 cup chilled water. Whisk well until all the sugar or salt has dissolved and all the lumps of yogurt are broken down, leaving a smooth flowing liquid. Stir in the coriander seeds and serve chilled, garnished with pistachio slivers.

Panna

Summer mango drink

This drink is popular all over Gujarat and Rajasthan. Green mangoes are very sour, which is why you add sugar and cardamom. This sweet-and-sour effect is great for boosting energy.

Serves 4

4 green mangoes
¹/₂ cup brown sugar, or to taste
¹/₂ teaspoon salt
1 teaspoon ground cardamom

Place the mangoes in a pan with some water and bring to a boil; simmer for about 30 minutes. Leave to cool, then remove from the pan. Peel, seed, and put the pulp into a bowl.

In a separate pan, bring the sugar and 1 cup water to a boil. When the sugar has dissolved, add the mango pulp and continue to cook for about 10 minutes. When it starts to thicken, remove from the heat and add the salt and cardamom. Dilute with chilled water and serve over ice.

Badaami karboocha

Almond and melon milk

This wonderful drink is invigorating, as well as delicious. Sunflower seeds are an excellent pick-me-up and this drink will give you energy.

Serves 4

6 tablespoons melon seeds or sunflower seeds
1 tablespoon white poppy seeds
1¹/₄ quarts milk
10 saffron strands
2 tablespoons honey or jaggery
1 tablespoon cashew nuts, chopped
1 tablespoon almonds, chopped
3 green cardamom pods, ground (with husks)
pinch of black pepper

Soak the melon or sunflower seeds in water for 30 minutes. Drain and place in a blender with the poppy seeds and 1 tablespoon of the milk.

Soak the saffron strands in about 1 tablespoon of hot water for 5 minutes. Heat the milk, then add the remaining ingredients to the pan. Stir in the sunflower seed mixture together with the saffron-infused water. Serve chilled.

Nimbu paani

Sweet lime water

This refreshing drink is served all over India during the summer. It is often served as a welcome drink.

Serves 4

¹/₃ cup sugar
juice of 1 lime
¹/₂ teaspoon salt
fresh mint and lemon slices, to garnish

Mix 3 cups water and the sugar together in a bowl until the sugar has dissolved. Add the lime juice and salt and stir well. Serve with ice and fresh mint leaves and lemon slices.

◇ **My tip** Squeezing fresh limes can be hard work. I put mine in the microwave for 10 seconds before squeezing them—it makes it much easier.

Menu suggestions

Vegetarian

Menu 1

Adraki gobi	Cauliflower with ginger (page 80)
Dal makhni	Lentils with cream and butter (page 106)
Paratha	Flaky bread (page 99)
	Plain basmati rice (page 97)

Menu 2

Gobi mutter	Cauliflower with green peas (page 81)
Paneer makhani	Indian cheese in a creamy tomato sauce (page 89)
Chappati	Indian flat bread (page 98)

Menu 3

Khumbh palak	Spicy stir-fried mushrooms and spinach (page 86)
Doodhi chana dal	Pumpkin and chickpeas (page 108)
Sada puri	Deep-fried puffed bread (page 102)

Menu 4

Batata nu saak	Spicy potatoes in a tomato sauce (page 82)
Dal triveni	Three-lentil dal (page 108)
Paneer chaman	Indian cheese in a mint and cilantro sauce (page 88)
Methi thepla	Chickpea flour pancakes with fenugreek (page 100)
Shaki tukra	Fried bread steeped in milk (page 117)

Special occasion

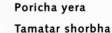

Poricha yera	Spiced fried shrimp (page 35)
Tamatar shorbha	Tomato soup (page 43)
Dal triveni	Three-lentil dal (page 108)
Khumbh palak	Spicy stir-fried mushrooms and spinach (page 86)
Achaari gosht	Lamb in a pickled spice sauce (page 74)
Dhaniya murgh	Cilantro chicken (page 60)
Dindigul biryani	Vegetable biryani (page 84)
Rabadi	Strawberry milk dessert (page 118)
Shrikhand	Creamy saffron yogurt (page 114)

Non-vegetarian

Menu 1

Tawa murgh   Chicken with fenugreek (page 58)

Bhendi aur aloo masala subzi Okra and potatoes (page 88)

Dal triveni   Three-lentil dal (page 108)

                                  Plain basmati rice (page 97)

Menu 2

Saagwala murgh   Chicken with spinach (page 63)

Batata nu saak   Spicy potatoes in a tomato sauce (page 82)

Punjabi chole   Chickpea curry (page 105)

Jeera pular   Rice flavored with cumin seeds (page 97)

Menu 3

Kozhi kurumelagu   Black pepper chicken (page 62)

Sambhar   South Indian lentil curry (page 106)

Beans poriyal   Green beans with coconut (page 91)

Tayir sadam   Yogurt with rice (page 96)

Kesan phirnee   Ground rice pudding with saffron milk (page 114)

Menu 4

Irachi varthathu   Dry-fried lamb with spices (page 71)

Chingri malai curry   Shrimp in a coconut cream sauce (page 51)

Dal makhni   Lentils with cream and butter (page 106)

Thengai pachadi   Coconut and yogurt dip (page 111)

                                  Plain basmati rice (page 97)

Party buffet

Pyaaz ke bhajie   Onion bhajias (page 32)

Khumbh ka shorbha   Kashmiri mushroom soup (page 42)

Dal makhni   Lentils with cream and butter (page 106)

Makai jalfrezi   Baby corn jalfrezi (page 86)

Saagwala murgh   Chicken with spinach (page 63)

Chingri malai curry   Shrimp in a coconut cream sauce (page 51)

Gosht biryani   Layered lamb biryani (page 72)

Shaki tukra   Fried bread steeped in milk (page 117)

Index

Acknowledgments

Very special thanks go to:

Lucie Morran for making it all happen and for her dedication throughout; Alison Cannon, who finally convinced me to write this book; Sunil Menon for helping me with the styling and food photography; my mother, Hansa Desai, for encouraging me to learn to cook; my parents-in-law, L.G. and Shanta Pathak, for helping me to understand the intricacies of East African Indian cooking; my belated cook, who trusted me with his recipes; both my grandmothers, Sumitra Desai and Mangla Desai, who loved eating and for whom I loved to cook; Kuntal Desai, who helped with all the location shots and travel arrangements in India; John Freeman for taking such beautiful photographs for the book; Roger Hammond for designing the book; Julie Saunders for helping me organize my diary and despite my hectic travel schedule managed to type out all the recipes for me; the Patak's Foods New Product Development kitchen, where I tested the recipes; Jet Travel in India. Last but not least, I must thank, at New Holland, my publisher, Yvonne McFarlane, and my editor, Clare Sayer, for their many hours of patient work.

The publishers would like to thank the following for providing props and food for photography:

Banwait Bros
75–77 The Broadway
Southall
Middlesex UB1 1LA
Tel: 020 8574 2635

The Cloth Shop
290 Portobello Road
London W10 5TE
Tel: 020 8968 6001

The Conran Shop
Michelin House
81 Fulham Road
London SW3 6RD
Tel: 020 7589 7401

Graham and Green
4,7 & 10 Elgin Crescent
London W11 2JA
Tel: 020 7727 4594

Liberty
210-220 Regent Street
London W1R 6AH
Tel: 020 7734 1234

Muji
Branches nationwide
Tel: 020 7287 7323

Neal Street East
5 Neal Street
London WC2
Tel: 020 7240 0135

Neelam Saris
388-390 Romford Rd
London E7
Tel: 020 8472 2410

The Pier
200 Tottenham Court Road
London W1P 7PL
Tel: 020 7436 9642

Sandy's Fishmongers
56 King Street
Middlesex
TW1 3SH
Tel: 020 8892 5788

David Wainwright
63 Portobello Road
London W11 3DB
Tel: 020 7727 0707

First published in paperback in 2005 by
New Holland Publishers (UK) Ltd
London · Cape Town · Sydney · Auckland

Garfield House
86 – 88 Edgware Road
London W2 2EA
United Kingdom
www.newhollandpublishers.com

80 McKenzie Street
Cape Town 8001
South Africa

14 Aquatic Drive
Frenchs Forest, NSW 2086
Australia

218 Lake Road
Northcote, Auckland
New Zealand

ISBN 1 84330 997 1

Project Editor: Clare Sayer
American Editor: Beverly LeBlanc
Patak's Development Chef: Sunil Menon
Design: Roger Hammond
Photographer: John Freeman
Assistant photographer: Alex Dow
Stylist: Labeena Ishaque
Production: Hazel Kirkman
Editorial Direction: Yvonne McFarlane

1 3 5 7 9 10 8 6 4 2

Reproduction by Pica Digital PTE Ltd, Singapore
Printed and bound by Times Offset (M) Sdn. Bhd., Malaysia

The Patak's story

MEENA PATHAK is the Director of Product Development for the authentic Indian food brand, Patak's. Patak's grew from very modest beginnings and is now the number one worldwide Indian food brand—a household name, used by professional chefs and home cooks across the world.

Patak's was founded in the late 1950s by L.G. Pathak, Meena's father-in-law, following his arrival in England with his wife and children. L.G. experienced great difficulty in finding employment and as a means to survive, he began making and selling Indian samosas and snacks from his home. They were well received and soon he had raised sufficient capital to buy his first small shop in North London. The business expanded with the introduction of other authentic Indian products, including pickles and chutneys; and orders flooded in.

Kirit Pathak joined the family business when he was forced to leave his studies at the age of 17 as the business had taken a turn for the worse. Meena herself became involved in Patak's shortly after her marriage to Kirit in 1976, when Kirit realized her creative cooking abilities. Having tasted a particularly delicious dish she had cooked for the family one evening he asked her, "Can you get that into a jar?," and her career in recipe and product development took off from there.

Throughout the 70s and 80s, the business prospered under Kirit and Meena's guidance. The product portfolio was extended to include pappadums and other Indian accompaniments and, in addition to supplying the Indian restaurant trade with pastes and chutneys, Patak's began exporting its range across the world into mainstream grocery markets.

Meena believes the key to a successful Indian dish is not just the distinctiveness of the recipe, but also the quality and freshness of the herbs, spices, and ingredients used. Because of this, Kirit personally supervizes the importation of the key ingredients from India and around the world. The herbs and spices are then ground at the factory in a unique grinding system, which guarantees the ingredients are as fresh as possible. The spice blends that form the basis of every Patak's recipe are known only to the members of the Pathak family.

The company's range has extended over the years from pickles and chutneys, to pastes and cooking sauces in jars and cans, ready-to-heat meals, pappadums, Indian breads, and now includes Indian snacks and frozen and chilled meals.

Patak's products are now widely available, enabling consumers to replicate their favorite Indian meals at home.

For more information on the company, visit the web site at www.pataks.co.uk